THE HISTORY OF
JASPER

Meghan Power

Summerthought

Banff, Alberta

THE HISTORY OF JASPER

Published by

Summerthought

Summerthought Publishing
PO Box 2309
Banff, AB T1L 1C1
Canada
www.summerthought.com

1st Edition – 2012; reprinted 2021

Editor: Rachel Small
Design and production: Linda Petras
Printed in Canada by Friesens

We gratefully acknowledge the financial support of the Alberta Foundation for the Arts for our publishing activities.

This project was funded in part by the
Alberta Historical Resources Foundation.

Library and Archives Canada Cataloguing in Publication
Power, Meghan, 1976-
The history of Jasper / Meghan Power.

(Canadian Rockies history: the series)
Includes bibliographical references and index.
ISBN 978-1-926983-00-4

1. Jasper (Alta.)—History. I. Title. II. Series: Canadian Rockies history: the series

FC3699.J39P68 2011   971.23'32   C2011-900687-1

Table of Contents

Introduction

Each year, two million people from all over the world visit Jasper National Park. They arrive by train, car, bus, and even bike to explore one of the world's greatest national parks. Their days are filled with activities as varied as hiking and golfing while in the evening they dine in world-class restaurants and stay in accommodations as varied as rustic hostels and the iconic Jasper Park Lodge.

But the worldwide acclaim and modern luxuries are relatively new. Long before Europeans arrived in what is now Jasper National Park, Aboriginal people hunted in grassland meadows of the Athabasca River Valley. These first people lived simply and left few clues of their nomadic lifestyle, although various archaeological excavations within the park have unearthed artefacts dated at up to 8000 years old. One of the earliest Europeans to pass through the valley was David Thompson, who in 1811 crossed Athabasca Pass. This was the beginning of a flood of fur traders, explorers, and surveyors to visit the area. In 1813, a fur trading post was established along the Athabasca River. Over the next century, the post was moved to Jasper Lake and was managed by a string of

One of the earliest known photos of Jasper House.

A railway construction camp near Jasper Lake.

men affiliated with the Hudson's Bay and North West companies, including Jasper Haws, whose name would eventually become associated with the park and town. In anticipation of the arrival of Canada's second transcontinental rail line, Jasper Forest Park was created in 1907 and when the railhead reached the Athabasca River Valley the remote settlement of Fitzhugh took hold. After being renamed Jasper, the town expanded steadily as the first tourists were transported into the wilderness by train. Over the ensuing decades, wealthy train tourists were joined in Jasper by families arriving by automobile and staying in campgrounds and bungalow camps. The Jasper of today enjoyed by locals and visitors alike is a place that has seen many changes over the last century, but at its heart remains as a welcoming resort town surrounded by some of the world's most magnificent scenery.

While enjoying the natural wonders and modern conveniences of Jasper, it is worth reflecting on this past, which is intimately linked to the town and park enjoyed today. The Jasper Yellowhead Historical Society, formed in 1963, has been a leader in the preservation of Jasper's past through the collection of stories,

Outdoor recreation has been an important part of Jasper's history.

images, and artefacts. The society's Jasper Yellowhead Museum is a wonderful resource, but this indoor attraction is just a starting point for a journey through local history. Near the museum is the former home of one of Jasper's best known residents, Fred Brewster, while the road between the museum and downtown passes by a number of other historic homes and the 1924 Our Lady of Lourdes Catholic Church. Downtown, one can enjoy a drink at the historic Athabasca Hotel, take in a movie at Jasper's original theatre, or visit the home of the first superintendent (now the Park Information Centre). While Jasper's many bungalow camps are regularly revamped, this form of accommodation is a great way to experience the park as visitors have done for generations. Further afield, you can enjoy the park's history by riding the Jasper Tramway, taking a boat tour on Maligne Lake, or saddling up for a backcountry horseback trip. For the really adventurous, a gruelling hike follows the path of David Thompson to remote Athabasca Pass.

Regardless of whether you are a lifelong resident or a first-time visitor, we hope you find this book the perfect companion to enhancing your time in Jasper National Park.

The Park Visitor Centre is the best known of Jasper's many historic buildings.

1 Origins

Although the story of Jasper begins in 1813 with the establishment of a trading post, the history of humans in the Athabasca River Valley dates back thousands of years.

Near the end of the last Ice Age, around 12,000 years ago, what is now Jasper National Park was an uninhabited, cold, and unforgiving region covered by a sheet of ice that extended across the Athabasca River Valley. As a warming trend began, the sheet of ice began receding northward, and megafauna such as mammoths, bison (also called buffalo), and huge bighorn sheep, as well as caribou, elk, deer, wolves, and bears, migrated into the Valley from the east. These animals were closely followed by Paleo-Indian hunters, who at first came in waves from the south and the east and formed several broad groups; many smaller bands, each with distinct cultures and languages, formed within these groups.

Study of Jasper's earliest human visitors has been a relatively recent phenomena, with the first archeological digs taking place in the 1960s. Evidence found by archeologists suggests the first humans to pass through what is now Jasper National Park did so around 10,000 years ago. It is thought that these earliest hunter-gatherers were highly mobile and travelled long distances across the plains and over mountain passes to trade, hunt big game, and quarry rock for tools and weapons. Obsidian flakes, unearthed at a dig site on the shoreline of Patricia Lake, were one of the most interesting discoveries made; the source of the flakes was traced to distant Mount Edziza in northwestern British Columbia—proof that travel and trade took place in the Athabasca River Valley many thousands of years ago.

Aside from Patricia Lake and pictographs at remote Devona Cave, most archeological discoveries have been made along the Athabasca River. The location for setting up camp would have been ideal—it was beside a source of fresh water, and the flat, open spaces along the river attracted large game such as sheep and deer.

Although it is not known exactly how the earliest nomadic hunter-gatherers reached the Athabasca River Valley, two theories are given credence by archaeologists. The first suggests

The distinctive profile of Roche Miette

Roche Miette

The origin of the name Roche Miette, an imposing peak that marks the transition from foothills to mountains northeast of town, goes back to the fur-trading era. According to legend, Miette was a voyageur who climbed to the summit and then sat with his feet dangling over the edge while he enjoyed his pipe. As historians have yet to find any record of a voyageur named Miette, the more logical origin of the name is the Cree word "my-a-tuck," which translates as "mountain sheep" (bighorn sheep are often seen by the highway at the base of the mountain).

they followed an ice-free corridor between the Cordilleran and Laurentide ice sheets that covered much of Canada at the time. The other theory suggests that the first North Americans used crude boats to follow the Pacific coastline. It is possible that early people used both routes to travel from the Beringia land bridge, which linked Alaska and Asia during the Ice Age, south onto the plains before spreading out and, over generations, moving northward as the ice age ended.

The Clovis, prehistoric Paleoindian hunters first identified at a bison kill site in Clovis, New Mexico, in the mid-1930s were for many years believed to have been the first inhabitants of North America, colonizing it from via the Beringia land bridge some 12,000 years ago. New research is proving the Clovis were not the first human beings to reach North America. The Clovis, who are known for their distinctive fluted spear points, were highly successful big game hunters. As they spread through the continent's western regions, the Clovis hunted bison, bighorn sheep, caribou, and mammoths.

About 10,500 years ago, it appears the Clovis were replaced by a culture known as the Folsom. It is unknown whether or not the Folsom were actually the Clovis with a more evolved culture and improved hunting tools. What is known, however, is that each subsequent culture developed increasingly sophisticated technological groups, which are referred to as phases, periods, or traditions, that replaced one another throughout North America's early history all the way to the time of the arrival of the Europeans.

Some of the most frequent visitors to the Athabasca River Valley were the Assiniboine, which means "people who cook with stones" (Europeans translated Assiniboine as "Stone People," or "Stoney"). The Assiniboine are a splinter group of the Sioux nation. They began moving north into present-day Canada in the mid-1600s. For generations, smaller groups slowly pushed northward then westward along the Saskatchewan River system; these groups became allies with the Cree, but kept their own identity, and pushed through the Blackfoot territory of the Plains to reach the Foothills approximately 200 years ago. They split into bands as they moved north and south along the Foothills and penetrated valleys where hunting was productive, such as the Athabasca River Valley. Moving with the seasons, they lived in small family-like groups and diversified their skills; they became excellent hunters of mountain animals, gathered berries in fall, and became less dependent on bison.

Before the arrival of the Europeans in North America, the Cree had inhabited most of eastern Canada for thousands of years. As fur traders pushed westward from Hudson Bay, the Cree followed;

they displaced enemies and adapted to new environments. By 1800, the Cree had moved as far west as Peace River. Although the Cree settled mostly in the forests fringing the prairies, splinter groups such as the Mountain Cree extended their territory into the mountainous regions of the Canadian Rockies. The Cree often acted as middlemen between the Europeans and Aboriginal groups, who were seeking furs and trading bison hides obtained from Plains people for European goods.

The Blackfoot covered a large territory that extended from what is now southern Saskatchewan all the way to the Canadian Rockies. Traditional prairie dwellers, they were the most warlike and feared of all the Aboriginal groups in western Canada. Linguistically linked to the Algonkians, before the arrival of the Europeans, the Blackfoot Confederacy comprised three allied bands: the Blackfoot (best known today as Siksika), who lived along the North Saskatchewan River; the Blood, along the Red Deer River; and the Peigan, along the Bow River. These bands spoke dialects of the Algonkian language, shared social and religious customs, and even hunted and camped together.

At various periods of time, the Sarcee, Beaver, and Sekani also travelled to the Athabasca River Valley in search of food and to trade. Traditionally, the Sarcee laid claim to the area between the Peace and Red Deer rivers. They divided from the subarctic Beaver in the mid-1800s and integrated with the Blackfoot through marriage and in customs and lifestyle, but they retained their Athabascan linguistic stock.

In the 1790s, around the time the first fur trading forts in Edmonton were established, the Beaver, who lived to the north of the North Saskatchewan River, separated into two groups. One group remained along the Peace River while the second group moved westward into the mountains via the Smoky River. The Sekani ("People of the rocks") lived mostly on the west side of the Continental Divide across the northern expanse of what is now British Columbia, but travelled frequently to and through the Athabasca River Valley. Closely related to the Beaver, the Sekani

Snake Massacre

Legend tells that in 1810, the Snake, a small band of Aboriginal people, were camped beside the Athabasca River. Their camp was not far from a much larger camp that belonged to their long-time enemies, the Assiniboine. The Assiniboine sent a message of peace and requested a meeting, but it was a ruse, and all but three young Snake women were killed. The three women were held captive until a Métis man named Bellerose snuck into the tepee where they were bound with rope, and set them free. Under the cover of night, the women fled up the river towards the mountains. One of the women survived the winter by herself before being discovered by an Iroquois man who had heard the story of the massacre and realized that she must be one of the survivors. He took her to his camp, and once she realized that they meant no harm, she stayed at the camp for two years before moving down to Jasper House.

The Snake Indian River, a tributary of the Athabasca River, is named for the Snake people, as is the remote Snake Indian Falls and equally remote Snake Indian Pass.

were known for their snare hunting skills. Their dress was unique in that they used porcupine quills to decorate their clothing. Due to their nomadic history, their social structure was less formal compared to other, more organized, western nations.

Evidence also suggests Shuswap, Kootenay, and Carrier people regularly crossed the Continental Divide from the west to hunt bison and to trade. Written records from the fur-trading era tell of a small band of Shuswap, whose territory extended from Lillooet to the Columbia River Valley, that lived in the Athabasca River Valley; artist Paul Kane noted in his journal that a Shuswap man made him a pair of snowshoes. The primary territory of the Carrier was the Cariboo region, also west of the Continental Divide.

By the mid-1700s, Aboriginal people throughout the region were beginning to feel the influence of the fur trade through disease and introduced goods, such as guns and horses. For the first time in thousands of years, Aboriginal people were forced to alter their traditional ways of life.

Eventually, tensions emerged between the local Aboriginal people and the Europeans regarding hiring eastern First Nations for guiding through the western plains and Canadian Rockies. The fur trade companies cited these eastern groups as having advanced skills in the use of modern steel traps and firearms. Further tension emerged due to the language and cultural barriers between company employees and the various Aboriginal groups living throughout the region. Eventually, the companies saw the advantage of having employees that could communicate with other groups. For example, the Cree were able to trade and communicate with the Kootenay and the Shuswap and were familiar with protocol and customs in these groups; they were therefore able to avoid insult and injury. The Cree would then trade the goods obtained from other groups with the fur trading posts. It was this entrepreneurial spirit that made the Athabasca River Valley a key junction for a trade route that relied on three of Canada's most important waterways—the Columbia, Athabasca, and North Saskatchewan rivers.

Numbered Treaties

In 1871, the first of 11 treaties was signed between the Government of Canada and the First Nations, many of whom had travelled to and through the Athabasca River Valley to hunt, gather, and trade. The government offered to provide land set aside as reserves for each nation, annual payments, and "a medicine chest . . . at the house of each Indian agent." Due to misunderstandings arising from poor translation and the fact that the Aboriginal people had no concept of or terms for land title, it is likely that they did not fully understand the agreements they had made. The Aboriginal nations believed they were signing peace treaties that would allow Europeans to live among them on the vast lands of what was then the North West Territories (including most of what is now Alberta). The Dominion of Canada and the British Crown, however, acknowledged the signing as total surrender. The government believed that negotiating and securing the surrender of the land was the only option available for opening the West to settlement and development.

2 Fur Trade

The first major catalyst for exploration and settlement across North America was the fur trade, which dates to the 1500s; fishermen from Europe would spend time ashore and trade knives with the Aboriginal people for beaver pelts. When the wide-brimmed hat came into fashion in the early 1600s, the demand for beaver pelts increased dramatically. In 1670, the Hudson's Bay Company had been granted a charter by King Charles II which gave the company a monopoly on trading rights for Rupert's Land, which comprised the entire 3.9 million square-kilometre drainage basin of Hudson Bay. By the mid-1700s, the Hudson's Bay Company and the North West Company had become intense rivals in a race to dominate the fur trade.

By the 1790s, the aggressive campaign for western expansion extended to what is now Alberta; both the Hudson's Bay and the North West companies built forts beside the North Saskatchewan River where the city of Edmonton now stands. Over the next two decades, the land west and northwest of Fort Edmonton was flooded with Iroquois trappers, voyageurs (fur traders who travelled by canoe), scientists, explorers, and the occasional independent traveller. Fur trade companies preferred to hire eastern First Nations, like the Iroquois, as trappers. The Iroquois made use of modern steel traps and fire arms, while local First Nations often relied on more traditional trapping methods. The modern traps and fire arms gave the Iroquois trappers a definite advantage.

The best-known and arguably the most important explorer to travel through the Athabasca River Valley was David Thompson, an employee of the Hudson's Bay Company from 1784 until 1797, when he began working for the North West Company. Most historians agree that Thompson left the Hudson's Bay Company because he was unhappy with his job; it had come to be more administrative and less about mapping territory, which was Thompson's primary interest.

Fortunately for Thompson, the North West Company saw value in Thompson's mapping and surveying skills and hired him to do just that. Thompson's first task was to map and survey the

David Thompson

David Thompson (1770–1857), one of Canada's greatest explorers, was a quiet, courageous, and energetic man who drafted the first comprehensive and accurate map of western Canada. He arrived in Canada from England at the age of 14 and immediately began working as an apprentice clerk for the Hudson's Bay Company. With an inquisitive nature and a talent for wilderness navigation, he quickly acquired the skills of surveying and mapmaking. The Aboriginal people called him "Koo-koo-sint" ("The Man Who Looks at Stars").

Thompson led four major expeditions into what is now Alberta—the first for the Hudson's Bay Company and the last three for its rival, the North West Company. The best known one was the fourth, which took place from 1810–1811. During this expedition, he travelled up the Athabasca River Valley and discovered the Athabasca Pass through the Continental Divide.

In 1813, Thompson began working on a master map that covered the entire territory controlled by the North West Company. The map was four metres long and two metres wide and detailed 3.8 million square kilometres. On completion, it was hung out of public view in the Great Hall of the North West Company headquarters at Fort William, on the shore of Lake Superior. It was years later, after his death in 1857, that the map was "discovered" and Thompson became recognized as one of the world's greatest land geographers.

North West Company's posts in southern Manitoba (the Red River region) and in the United States. As a result, Thompson embarked on a journey that essentially led him to draw the first map of Canada. This chart was very important to the North West Company too, because it helped them locate and establish new trade routes, which would eventually give them the lead over the competition.

One of the new trade routes that Thompson established for his employer was over Athabasca Pass, which eventually became an essential link to the west coast. Traditionally, fur brigades (convoys of fur traders) used Howse Pass to cross the Continental Divide, but a triad of tension between the Peigan, the Kootenay, and David Thompson himself altered the course of Canadian history and travel. It is unknown if the Peigan and Kootenay were enemies prior to European contact, but what is certain is that the animosity increased considerably after the introduction of firearms. The Peigan were especially vigilant in the protection of their traditional territory. When they discovered that David Thompson had traded firearms with the Kootenay for goods, the Peigan were furious. It was understood to be a bold betrayal.

They blocked Thompson from accessing Howse Pass and threatened him with violence if he attempted to cross their blockade. Thompson, acutely aware of the Peigan's prowess in battle, was not interested in risking his life or the lives of his men. So began Thompson's search for another pass. Albertan historian James G. MacGregor noted that Thompson was made aware of the Athabasca Pass route by his Iroquois guide, Thomas, who had heard of its existence.

Thompson and his team of 24 men and 24 horses reached the Athabasca River near Obed Creek in late October 1810. On December 3, 1810, they reached an abandoned trapper's cabin at Brule Lake, a wide stretch of the Athabasca River northeast of present-day Jasper. Thompson then knew he was heading in the right direction as Thomas had mentioned "The Shack." With the onset of colder weather upon them, Thompson and his men decided to use the area as a base camp.

As the cabin was very small, Thompson and his men moved to the north end of Brule Lake and built another shelter to store provisions. Over the next three weeks they prepared for the adventure ahead by crafting rudimentary snowshoes and building toboggans to transport supplies.

When Thompson and his men set off up the frozen waters of the Athabasca River, they left William Henry at Brule Lake to protect the stored provisions and tend to the horses. Upon approaching Athabasca Pass, Thompson wrote, ". . . before us was an ascent of deep snow, in all appearance to the height of land between the Atlantic and Pacific Oceans, it was to me a most exhilarating sight, but to my uneducated men a dreadful site . . . the scene of desolation before us was dreadful, and I knew it, a heavy gale of wind much more a mountain storm would have buried us beneath it, but thank God the weather was fine." Thompson reached Athabasca Pass on January 10, 1811. It was a discovery that would play an important role in the fur trade and transportation across the Continental Divide for the next 40 years.

It had not been an easy expedition, and along the way, some of Thompson's men chose to return to Brule Lake and the stored provisions at what had become fondly known as Henry's House. By the time Thompson returned to the Athabasca River Valley, William Henry had realized that the original location was less than ideal for grazing horses due to a lack of grass. Although historians agree that Henry's original camp at Brule Lake was abandoned in 1812, to this day, they debate the location of the new Henry's House although many believe it was near the confluence of the Miette and Athabasca rivers.

Between 1813 and 1829, the Athabasca Pass was the primary route used by both the Hudson's Bay Company and the North West Company for delivering mail and supplies to their remote trading posts on the west side of the Continental Divide and for taking furs back over to the east side, where they were transported by river to the company's respective headquarters at York Factory and Lachine. As fur trade traffic increased, the North West Company established a trading post at the north end of Brule Lake, near the confluence of Solomon Creek. The post was ideally situated for Aboriginal people who were using Snake Indian Pass to the north. Completed in 1813 by Francois Decoigne, a North West Company employee, the new post became known as Rocky Mountain House (the same name was used for a post beside the North Saskatchewan River, further south). It was a place where traders and their horses could rest and replenish supplies before heading up and over the pass. Decoigne left the Athabasca River Valley the following summer and worked at Lesser Slave Lake before changing employers and moving to the Hudson's Bay Company post on Lake Athabasca.

Decoigne was replaced at Rocky Mountain House by Jasper Haws (also spelled Hawes). Modern-day descendants of Haws have traced him to Maryland, where he was born to United Empire Loyalists in 1770. Young Jasper and his family migrated to Sorel, Quebec, to avoid persecution for their loyalty to the British Crown during the American Revolution. In his mid-twenties, Haws travelled to Montreal and found employment with North West Company associates who were plying the waters of the Red and Missouri rivers. After 20 years of service with the North West Company, Haws, aged 44, was sent to the Athabasca River Valley to manage a post that would eventually be associated with his name; today, the town and national park also bear his name.

Jasper Haws managed the trading post for the next three years. In early June, 1817, fur trader Ross Cox rested at Jasper House. In his 1831 book *Adventures on the Columbia River*, Cox wrote of the remote post, "This building was a miserable concern of rough logs, with only three apartments, but scrupulously clean inside. An old clerk, Mr. Jasper Hawes [sic], was in charge and had under his command two Canadians, two Iroquois and three hunters." While at this post, Jasper married an Iroquois woman, and the couple had five children.

When the North West and Hudson's Bay companies amalgamated in 1821, Haws was left without work. He returned to Quebec and lived on a farm in the Chateauguay Valley until his death in 1855.

After the North West and Hudson's Bay companies amalgamated, the Council of the Northern Department of Rupert's Land, under the advisement of Hudson's Bay Company governor George Simpson, appointed Joseph Felix Larocque to establish a post near the Yellowhead Pass at Cranberry Lake (now known as Yellowhead Lake). Believing that Cranberry Lake was not an ideal location to initiate trade, Larocque made an executive decision and constructed the post closer to Jasper House. The location Larocque chose was near the present-day east entrance to the town of Jasper. Despite the new trading post being described as a "neat little group of wood huts . . ." and its inhabitants as "cheerful and happy," George Simpson was displeased that Larocque had broken rank and disobeyed his order. He closed Larocque's post just one year after it had been completed.

In 1824, the Hudson's Bay Company sent Michel Klyne to Jasper House as its new postmaster. Klyne, described by fellow Hudson's Bay Company employee Alexander Ross as a "jolly fellow with a large family," was born in Quebec and began working with the North West Company as a voyageur in the 1790s. He and his Métis wife, Suzanne Lafrance, raised 10 children at Jasper House, including a son, George, who went on to be elected to the Legislative Assembly of Manitoba. By 1829, Klyne had decided that Jasper House was too far away from the action, and he relocated the post from Brule Lake to Jasper Lake.

Throughout his tenure in the Athabasca River Valley, Klyne kept detailed records of the trading he did with the local Iroquois, Shuswap, and other settlers who lived at the abandoned post built by Larocque. Between 1827 and 1830, Klyne recorded taking in 1594 beaver pelts. The names of the men that he traded with

Who were the Métis?

The exact definition of "Métis" (from the Latin word miscere, meaning "to mix") varies across Canada, but the term originated in the 1700s to describe those born of a mixed racial heritage as a result of relationships between French or Scottish fur traders and Cree, Ojibwa, and Salteaux women. The Métis played an invaluable role in the fur trade because they were bilingual and also able to perform traditional tasks such as skinning animals and tanning hides. By the early 1800s, a distinct Métis culture developed along trading routes. As the fur trade ended, many Métis found themselves drawn towards the familiarity of their own people and remained together in areas such as the Athabasca River Valley. The largest group of Métis was concentrated along central Canada's Red River. Government threats to take their Red River land led to the 1869 Riel Rebellion and the 1885 North West Rebellion, after which the displaced Métis drifted westward to what is now northern Alberta; here, they eked out food by hunting, trapping, and fishing. Although the Métis were granted land in 12 different locations across Alberta in 1936, for generations they were a people stuck between two cultures; they were excluded from treaties signed by full-blooded Aboriginal people but were not part of mainstream Canadian society.

The Wicked River

The Maligne River was named by Belgian priest Father Pierre-Jean De Smet, who is best remembered for convincing Sioux war chief Sitting Bull to participate in treaty negotiations with the United States government in 1868. Prior to this, he travelled extensively through western North America. De Smet's longest journey, which began in 1845, took him up the Columbia River and over White Man Pass on a peace mission involving the Blackfoot Nation. After a summer on the Canadian plains, he spent the winter at Fort Edmonton and then set off in the spring of 1846 for Jasper House to perform baptisms and marriages for the Iroquois who had settled in the Athabasca River Valley. During this phase of his trip, De Smet noted the strong current at the confluence of two rivers in his journal and called the waters "maline," a French word for "wicked" or "treacherous." The name "Maligne" was eventually used for not only the river but also for the lake, canyon, pass, mountain, and mountain range.

Father Pierre-Jean De Smet

include the following: Jacques (Jacco) Findlay, James Findlay, Louis Loyer, Antoine Cardinal, Antoine Auger, and Pincheas Findlay. Another important visitor to Jasper House during Klyne's tenure was Thomas Drummond, a botanist who was part of an overland expedition to the Arctic coast led by John Franklin. In 1826, independently of the expedition, he travelled as far west as Athabasca Pass and collected over 1,000 botanical specimens as well as recording various birds and mammals, including the first record of a ptarmigan. In 1831, his findings were published in the book *Fauna Boreali-Americana*. Klyne left Jasper House in 1834 and retired near central Canada's Red River.

After Klyne's retirement, Colin Fraser was sent to run Jasper House. Born in Scotland in 1807, Fraser was first hired as George Simpson's personal piper during his 1828 journey to New Caledonia (British Columbia). Simpson was a difficult boss and wrote of his disappointment in Fraser's piping abilities: "We are getting along steadily considering the state of the Water & the Weakness of some of our Men . . . the Piper cannot find sufficient Wind to fill his Bag . . . Colin breaks in by degrees I rub him against the grain as frequently as worth, he is a piper and nothing but a piper." Despite Simpson's earlier doubts regarding Fraser's fortitude, Fraser moved up the ranks of the Hudson's Bay Company from piper to interpreter, and in 1835, he was promoted to the position of postmaster at Jasper House.

During the winter months, food was scarce at Jasper House and had to be rationed among Fraser, his Métis wife, their nine children, and any workers that happened to be staying there. Winter was not an easy season for hunting, and Métis hunters and local freemen prepared for the long winter ahead in the fall. Meat from bighorn sheep was a winter staple, and moose, caribou, porcupine, hare, beaver, muskrat, duck, pheasant, owl, and whitefish were all considered delicacies. During the winter, the postmaster also had to protect his herds from wolves and make sure that there was enough pasture for his horses to graze.

Even though supplies were sparse at Jasper House, there were some luxuries available that made the hard life a little more enjoyable. Luxury items such as tea (probably the most popular luxury trade item), pimento, chocolate, pepper, salt, mustard, and sugar were saved for special occasions like Christmas.

During his 15-year tenure at Jasper House, Fraser interacted freely with other families who had settled in the valley, including the Decoignes, Findlays, Wards, Chalifouxs, and Desjarlais. One of the most well-known families living in the Athabasca River Valley during Fraser's time was the Karakonti family (the spelling of the family surname has many variations, including Kwarakwante and Karquienthe). Of Iroquois descent, Louis Karakonti travelled west as a voyageur with the North West Company around 1800 when in his late teens. Known as "le voyageur de soleil" (Sun Traveller), he met a Sekani woman, Marie Katis, at Jasper House. The couple had many children, including Louis Dekara. Although records show that the elder Louis spent the latter years of his life trapping on the Smoky River near Grande Cache, he returned to Jasper often.

Visitors who enjoyed Fraser's hospitality during his tenure at Jasper House included some of the first missionaries to visit western Canada: Fathers Francois Blanchette and Modeste Boniface (1838) and Belgian priest Father Pierre-Jean De Smet (1846), who baptized and married the Iroquois families who had by this time settled around Jasper House.

Another important visitor to stay at Jasper House was the great Canadian artist Paul Kane. The diary Kane kept during his travels includes written commentary regarding the places that he visited and the people whom he met, as well as sketches of the landscape he encountered. This was the first time any artistic rendering was made of specific landscapes, such as the area around Jasper House.

Paul Kane

Paul Kane (1810–1871) was an Irish-born artist who at a young age moved to Toronto with his family. In 1841, he travelled throughout Europe and learned to paint by carefully studying European masters. Upon his return to British North America (Canada), Kane set off to capture on canvas what he described as the "disappearing Indian." In a two-and-a-half-year journey that took him across the continent, he returned with over 700 sketches, hundreds of artifacts, and a diary filled with his observations of the Aboriginal people. His travels culminated in the 1859 publication *Wanderings of an Artist*, in which he describes an incident along the Athabasca River:

The Indians here do not number above fifteen or twenty; they are the Shoo-chwap [sic] tribe, and their chief, of whom I made a sketch, is called "Capote Blanc" by the voyageurs—in their own language it is Assannitchay, but means the same. His proper location is a long distance to the north east; but he had been treacherously entrapped, whilst traveling with thirty seven of his people, by a hostile tribe, which met him and invited him to sit down and smoke a pipe of peace. They unsuspectingly laid down their arms, but before they had time to smoke their treacherous hosts seized their arms and murdered them all except eleven who managed to escape, and fled to Jasper's House, where they remained, never daring to return to their own country through the hostile tribe. Capote Blanc was a very simple, kind-hearted old man, with whom I became very friendly.

Paul Kane's 1847 sketch of Jasper House.

Kane's diary includes the following description of Jasper House: "November 4th—Jasper's house consists of only three miserable log huts. The dwelling house is composed of two rooms, of about fourteen or fifteen feet square each. One of them is used by all comers and goers: Indians, voyageurs, and traders, men, women, and children being huddled together indiscriminately; the other room being devoted to the exclusive occupation of Colin and his family, consisting of a Cree squaw and nine interesting half-breed children. One of the huts is used for storing provisions in, when they can get any, and the other I should have thought a dog kennel had I seen many of the canine species about. This post is only kept up for the purpose of supplying horses to parties crossing the mountains." Kane's diary was later published in book form as *Wanderings of an Artist*, and to this day, his sketches deliver a unique view of life from Jasper House and, at the same time, a grand view of Canada in its infancy.

Colin Fraser left Jasper House in 1850 when he was transferred to Fort Assiniboine; he remained here until 1853, at which time he moved to Lac St. Anne, but Fraser's bloodline lived on in the Athabasca River Valley. In 1861, one of his daughters, Madeline, married Alexis Joachim, whose Iroquois father had travelled west

Father Albert Lacombe

Father Albert Lacombe (1827–1916), who typically brandished a cross and dressed in a tattered black robe, dedicated his life to those with Aboriginal blood. His reputation extended to every corner of what is now the province of Alberta; he was a spokesman for the Church, an effective influence on government policies, and, most importantly, he was involved in almost every advance in the often-tense relationship between the Aboriginal people and Europeans.

Ordained as a priest in 1849, he travelled throughout the region from his mission at Lac Ste. Anne between 1853 and 1861. Lacombe's first recorded visit to Jasper House was in 1853, when he presided over the marriage of Louis Karakonti and Marie Katis.

In 1861, Lacombe founded a mission at what is now St. Albert (northwest of Edmonton) and continued to travel widely; he instigated Canada's first industrial school for Aboriginal people, mediated a dispute between the Canadian Pacific Railway and angry leaders of the Blackfoot over rights to build a rail line through their territory, and wrote the first Cree dictionary. Today, St. Albert's Father Lacombe Chapel is Alberta's oldest building, and the town of Lacombe is named in his honour.

from Montreal as an employee of the North West Company. The couple had eight children together. Their son Adam, who was educated by Father Albert Lacombe and fluent in four languages—English, Cree, French, and Latin—went on to have 17 children with two different wives. Although he was forced to abandon his Athabasca River Valley homestead when Jasper Forest Park was established in the early 1900s, Adam remained an important part of Jasper's history as a well-respected guide and packer and as a keeper of the park's history.

By the early 1850s, the Hudson's Bay Company had ordered that all furs collected on the west side of the Continental Divide be shipped to Fort Victoria, on the Pacific coast. As a result, voyageurs stopped at Jasper House far less frequently, and in 1857, George Simpson officially ordered the post closed; however, the families that had settled in the valley continued hunting, trapping, and trading in the area.

In late 1853, the Hudson's Bay Company hired an ambitious young man named Henry John Moberly to work as an apprentice clerk at La Cloche, on Lake Huron, from where he was transferred between a number of trading posts across what is now Alberta. When posted at Edmonton, he was asked by superiors to check on the status of Jasper House. From Fort Edmonton, he was guided by Andre Cardinal, a Métis who had been born in the Athabasca River Valley. Moberly reported that the post was in desperate need of repair: "[the buildings] had been long untenanted, badly needed repairing, the chinks between the logs re-mudding, the chimneys patching and the windows fitting with new parchment." He also recommended that the Hudson's Bay Company reopen Jasper House as there was a thriving community in the area and the possibility to make money. In 1858, when the Hudson's Bay Company placed Moberly in charge of the post, he repaired the buildings and re-established trade relations with the valley's inhabitants. During his time at Jasper House, Henry Moberly married Suzanne Karakonti, daughter of Louis Karakonti. The couple had two sons, Ewan and John. Moberly also returned to Fort Edmonton on occasion, including on May 19, 1861; journal records from this day state, ". . . nothing worth notice this day with the exception of the arrival of Mr Moberly's Men with the Jasper House returns. They have been very careless. Their packs are in very bad order."

In 1861, Henry Moberly left Jasper House for a position at Fort Fraser in northern British Columbia, where he worked until 1864. Over the next 30 years, he divided his time between Hudson's Bay Company posts throughout northern British Columbia and northern Alberta, while also taking leaves of absences, including in the 1860s when he spent time hunting and prospecting around Chetwynd (where Moberly Lake is named after him). Moberly officially retired in 1894 before passing away at the age of 97 in Duck Lake, Saskatchewan, in 1932. Meanwhile, his wife Suzanne remained in the Athabasca River Valley and raised their two sons.

Upon leaving the Athabasca River Valley in 1861, Moberly was replaced by Joseph Brazeau, who had begun his career in the fur trade along the Missouri River before finding employment with the Hudson's Bay Company. Brazeau had previously been posted to Jasper House in the early 1850s before being transferred to Rocky Mountain House. Married to Marguerite Brabant, the daughter of Métis leader Augustin Brabant, Brazeau's skills as an interpreter were highly regarded by John Palliser, leader of the Palliser Expedition, who stopped at Rocky Mountain House in 1859 and recorded that: "Mr. Brazeau had been for many years in the American fur trade; was a wonderful Indian linguist, and spoke Stoney, Sioux, Salteau, Cree, Blackfoot, and Crow—six languages, five of which are totally distinct from one another. Being of an old Spanish family, and educated in the United States, he also spoke English, French, and Spanish fluently."

Brazeau was replaced as Jasper House postmaster in 1862 by John McAulay, who had started his career with the Hudson's Bay Company at York Factory as an apprentice clerk in 1856. McAulay ran Jasper House for four years, during which time he married Mary Jane Brazeau, the daughter of a former postmaster. Over the next two decades, Jasper House was run by a variety of people, although records are incomplete: Joseph McDonald (1867 to 1868), John Rowland (1869), Charles Savage (1870), James Kirkness (1877), William Brereton (1880 to 1883), and William Leslie Wood (1884).

When the Hudson's Bay Company officially closed Jasper House in 1891, the two Moberly boys remained; they established homesteads that became important supply depots and rest stops for the new wave of explorers passing through the Athabasca River Valley. Other families, many with Métis heritage, also remained around the abandoned Jasper House. They included the descendants of Joseph Brazeau; Jacques (Jacco) Findlay, who is credited with the first crossing of Howse Pass; Hudson's Bay Company employee Colin Fraser, who was assigned Jasper House postmaster in 1835; and Louis Karakonti, one of the valley's first permanent settlers. Births and deaths recorded at Jasper House up to the early 1890s also include the following family names:

Barland, Beachamp, Berland, Blandion, Brazeau, Brosseau, Cardinal, Collins, Courtepatte, Gladu, Gray, Gullion, Ignace, Karakonti, L'Hirondelle, and Noyes.

Workers on the Grand Trunk Pacific Railway dismantled Jasper House in 1909 and used its timbers to build rafts. Today, there is no road access to the site, but a plaque along Highway 16 commemorates its important role in the fur trade and the settlement of the valley. The plaque is 35 kilometres northeast of Jasper, beyond the north end of Jasper Lake. The site of Jasper House is across the Athabasca River from this point.

Métis Beadwork

The Métis were recognized by their colourful and ornate style of dress, which was highlighted by unique beadwork patterns that appeared on much of their clothing.

The elaborate floral motif that is commonly seen in early Métis beadwork is an example of how the landscape influenced beading patterns. The most  popular flower depicted in Métis beadwork is the prairie rose, a common wildflower admired for its hardiness and seen as a sign of an early spring. Métis women were sometimes called prairie roses as a tribute to their beauty and hardiness. The floral motif became an expression of self-identification and honoured the land that provided them with food and shelter.

Beads used by Métis women were usually brightly coloured. Metallic beads were more expensive than glass beads and were not as easy to obtain, so they were used sparingly and as accents. Rough cut glass beads were also used to accentuate the pattern because they were more eye-catching.

Jackets worn by hunters were elaborately decorated by the hunters' wives, who also tanned and prepared the animal hides; some women would burn poplar trees and use the smoke to tan the hides. This gave the skins a pleasant smell. The designs on the jacket reflected the landscape and honoured hunted animals. It was believed that when the animals saw how beautiful their skins had become, they would acknowledge the honour and respect the Métis woman had for the precious hide.

3 Exploration

Aboriginal people had been travelling though what is now Jasper National Park for thousands of years before the first European, David Thompson, arrived in the early 1800s. While Thompson was the first European explorer on record to pass through what is now Jasper National Park, it must be assumed that the men who lived at Jasper House from 1813 onwards—Francois Decoigne, Jasper Haws, Colin Fraser, and Henry John Moberly—also spent time exploring the valley and its surrounds although no written records exist.

Few early visitors would have as much effect on western Canada as the three-year Palliser Expedition between 1857 and 1860. The purpose of this expedition was to evaluate the conditions on the southern Prairies to determine if the area was suitable for settlement and agriculture and to probe the mountains for a suitable pass through to British Columbia. The idea of linking British Columbia by rail with the rest of Canada was not new. The concept had been considered as early as the 1840s, but as the Hudson's Bay Company owned the drainage basin of the Hudson Bay, a vast territory then known as Rupert's Land that extended west to the Canadian Rockies, building a railway would be complicated. This did not mean, however, that Canada and Great Britain could not begin the groundwork for a link.

In 1857, the Royal Geographical Society of London, England, sent Irish landowner and explorer Captain John Palliser to British North America with a lofty mandate. At its heart, the society, and by extension Great Britain and the colonial government of Canada, wanted to affirm its ownership of Rupert's Land and the North West Territories. The society believed that settlement and a road, perhaps even a railroad, would help to accomplish that goal.

Members of the expedition led by Palliser included James Hector, a geologist and naturalist; Eugene Bourgeau, a botanist, John W. Sullivan, a secretary and astronomical observer; and Thomas Blakiston, a naturalist and astronomer.

The Palliser expedition arrived at Fort Edmonton in January 1859. That same month, expedition leader John Palliser sent Dr.

Captain John Palliser and geologist James Hector were members of the five-man Palliser expedition.

James Hector westward to explore the Athabasca River Valley by dog sled. Hector, a well-educated man, specialized in many fields, including medicine, geology, and biology. For 18 days, using Jasper House as a base and Henry Moberly as a local guide, Hector's group collected rock specimens from the valley and made topographical notes on the lay of the land. Hector travelled as far as the Whirlpool River, with this portion of his trip guided by Louis Karakonti and his son Dekara.

Another visitor in 1859 was James Carnegie, ninth Earl of Southesk. The earl was to be the first in a long line of tourists who would travel to the Rocky Mountains in pursuit of, as the earl said, " . . . an active open air life in a healthy climate." After travelling between New York and Fort Garry with Hudson's Bay Company president George Simpson, Carnegie continued on to

Earl of Southesk

Born in Edinburgh in 1827, James Carnegie, the ninth Earl of Southesk, was the first "tourist" to pass through what is now Jasper National Park.

Carnegie grew up in the privileged surroundings of Kinnaird Castle, Scotland, his family's ancestral home. In 1859, after the death of his first wife, he followed

the advice of his doctor and took an extended holiday to the Rocky Mountains for fresh air and sport. Although dressed in traditional Western buckskin, he was accompanied by an entourage that included a gamekeeper from his Scottish estate and an Iroquois cook.

The nature of mountain travel and hunting disappointed him. He describes the desolation of the mountains with harsh words that mirror his experiences. "The very mass and vastness of the mountains depress and daunt the soul; scarcely can you look up at the blue sky without some portentous object sternly frowning down your gaze," he wrote in his journals, which were

The Earl of Southesk

published in 1875 as *Saskatchewan and the Rocky Mountains: A diary and narrative of sport, and adventure, during a journey through the Hudson's Bay Company's territories in 1859 and 1860.*

Today, a lake, a pass, and two mountains within Jasper National Park are named in his honour, and Aboriginal artifacts collected on his trip are held by Edmonton's Royal Alberta Museum.

Fort Edmonton, where he purchased supplies for the rest of his journey. Although he had brought some necessities with him from home—his personal library of Shakespeare books, 100 pounds of his favourite tobacco, and an array of weapons—he rounded off his provisions with luxuries such as a portable bathtub. As a man of leisure, Carnegie obviously had little interest in roughing it during his Canadian vacation.

A chance meeting with Henry Moberly on the trail out to Jasper House led to a change of plans; Moberly informed the earl that the post had been hit with hard times and that game was scarce in the Athabasca River Valley. He advised the earl to travel up the McLeod River and over Rocky Pass to reach the South Saskatchewan River, a route that, as Moberly noted, "no European had ever seen." After crossing Rocky Pass, the earl and his party set up camp beside the Medicine Tent River. After climbing a nearby mountain via a pass that now bears his name, he wrote in his journal, "I am the first European who has visited this valley, and if I might have the geographic honour of giving my name to some spot of earth, I should choose the mountain near which the two rivers rise." From this point, Carnegie continued south to the Kootenay Plains and over Pipestone Pass to the Bow Valley. His journal is filled with descriptions of the landscapes he encountered, camp life, and descriptions of his party's often-bloody hunts. In his diary he also shares some of his more philosophical musings about hunting: "There is something repugnant to the feelings in carrying death and anguish on so large a scale amongst beautiful inoffensive animals."

The first large party to travel through the Athabasca River Valley during this period was the Overlanders, who passed through in the summer of 1862 in search of fortune at the Cariboo goldfields. The Overlanders had banded together after beginning their trek from Ontario as smaller groups of westward-bound gold seekers; the group numbered around 200 men by the time it reached Fort Edmonton. When dissention arose regarding the best route to take across the Rocky Mountains, the group split. The main party, which numbered around 115 and was led by Thomas McMicking, set off from Fort Edmonton on July 29, 1862; Andre Cardinal had been hired to guide them across the mountains. The journey was not easy; the carts and stubborn oxen were not well suited to the narrow, old trails and equally stubborn muskeg. After negotiating Disaster Point, they passed through the Athabasca River Valley along a route paralleling the river that is now known as the Overlander hiking trail. They crossed the treacherous lower reaches of the Maligne River, and then fought their way through thick forest up the Miette River Valley to Yellowhead Pass, descended along the Fraser River, and eventually reached Quesnel on September 11, 1862. By this time, most of the goldfields had been claimed and many of the original gold seekers were already leaving. As McMicking noted upon his arrival, "Our mining tools were the only articles that we found to be unnecessary." Although the Overlanders did not find riches at the goldfields, their journey proved that a legitimate travel route between British Columbia and the rest of Canada was possible.

Much like the Earl of Southesk, William Wentworth Fitz-william, a British aristocrat better known as Lord Milton, and Dr. Walter Cheadle arrived in Canada with grand plans to explore the Rocky Mountains. After resting at Jasper House early in the summer of 1863, they hired an Iroquois guide to take them up the Miette River Valley and over Yellowhead Pass to Tête Jaune Cache. From this crest of the pass, they followed the Fraser River to the Pacific Ocean. Upon returning to England, Lord Milton was given a seat in the House of Commons; Cheadle authored a book, *North-West Passage by Land* and was elected to the Royal Geographical Society.

A small community, many of them Métis families, remained in the Athabasca River Valley after Jasper House closed in 1891.

Ewan Moberly, son of Henry Moberly, married Madeleine Findlay and in 1897 the couple established a homestead south of Jasper House on the west side of the Athabasca River; here, they raised 10 children. Their son Adolphus, born in 1881, became a

John Moberly (right) standing behind his wife, Marie Joachim.

legendary guide and outfitter in the early 1900s. Ewan's brother, John, married Marie Joachim, Adam Joachim's sister, and between 1893 and 1909 they had six children together. In 1899, John and his growing family settled upstream from his brother on the east side of the Athabasca River. The Moberly men became well known for their local knowledge and hospitality. Their homesteads, positioned on either side of the river, became stopping places for travellers heading over the Yellowhead Pass and, with Jasper House closed, they traded furs with local trappers.

Meanwhile, in 1870, the Hudson's Bay Company sold Rupert's Land to the Canadian government for £300,000. The following year, in 1871, British Columbia joined Confederation; this decision was partly based on a promise made to British Columbia by the federal government to build a transcontinental railway. The information collected by Carnegie, the members of the Palliser Expedition, the missionaries, and the fur trade explorers formed a record, some of it illustrated by drawings and maps, that would provide the Canadian Pacific Railway (CPR) with reference material as the company set out to choose a route for the transcontinental railway. The CPR's chief engineer, Sir Sandford Fleming, took charge of the Canadian Pacific Survey in 1871, and by mid-summer, he had 800 men surveying potential routes for the railroad. Having read Dr. Cheadle's book, *North-West Passage by Land*, he was especially keen to have the Yellowhead Pass surveyed. One of the first members of the survey team to reach the Athabasca River Valley was Frank Moberly, whose brother Henry had operated Jasper House between 1858 and 1861. Frank was accompanied by Charles Horetzky, whose photographs are among the earliest taken of the Athabasca River Valley.

In 1872, Walter Moberly, who was another brother of Henry Moberly, surveyed a number of passes across the Continental Divide, including the Yellowhead and Athabasca passes. Walter Moberly had previously completed extensive survey work in British Columbia, which included laying out the streets of New Westminster and helping survey the Dewdney Trail and Cariboo Road.

Jasper House in 1872, as photographed by Charles Horetzky.

Fleming himself headed west with John Macoun, a botanist, and Reverend George Grant, a clergyman and close friend from Halifax. Grant worked as a secretary for Fleming, and his extensive writing includes the following description of the Athabasca River Valley: "It looks as if nature had united all her forces to make this the natural highway into the heart of the Rocky Mountains." Grant also describes Mount Edith Cavell, from his view on the valley floor, as "a great mountain, so white with snow that it [looks] like a sheet suspended from the heavens." The reverend is also credited with naming Roche à Perdrix (Partridge Rock) for its folded strata, which he thought resembled a partridge tail. Fleming and Walter Moberly met at Jasper House in September 1872 and described the abandoned house as "untenanted, locked, and shuttered."

In 1875, one of the railway surveyors working for Fleming, Henry McLeod (sometimes spelled MacLeod), followed the

Maligne River from the Athabasca River Valley to its source but found travelling up the Maligne Valley very difficult—when he reached the lake at the head of the valley, he dubbed it "Sore Foot," for his difficult journey. Not wanting to traverse the valley a second time, McLeod headed east and followed the Rocky River back to the Athabasca River Valley. Not surprisingly, upon returning to Edmonton, McLeod reported to Fleming that the Maligne Valley was not a practical route for the transcontinental railway—although he had made the official recording of arguably Jasper National Park's most recognizable natural feature—what is known today as Maligne Lake.

Pyramid Mountain

A Mountain Panorama

Impressive mountains surround the town of Jasper, each one with its own story to tell. Easily identifiable to the west are the twin peaks of The Whistlers. Although not particularly high (which may explain why nobody bothered to record the name of the first person to climb them), a tramway leading up their eastern face makes them one of the best-known destinations in Jasper National Park. In 1916, Edouard Deville, the Surveyor General of Canada, officially named them "The Whistlers" after the abundance of whistling marmots that make a home on the

By the end of 1876, the CPR had considered six passes through the Rocky Mountains and a total of twelve routes across the country. Fleming championed the Yellowhead Pass west of Jasper. He believed this pass was a good fit for the railway as construction would be easier and less costly due to its relatively low height and gentle gradient up the Miette River Valley. He wrote, "It is . . . undoubtedly established that the main Rocky Mountain chain can be crossed with ease by the Yellow Head Pass."

For a period of time, the Canadian government agreed with Fleming, and it appeared that the Athabasca River Valley would form an important link along the transcontinental rail line.

mountain. The year before, in 1915, a rough trail had been constructed to the summit. This demanding hike is usually bypassed, however, and most people board Jasper Tramway to easily reach the mountain summit.

To the south of The Whistlers is one of the most distinctive peaks in Jasper National Park: Mount Edith Cavell—the only peak within sight of town that is snow-capped year-round. Cavell was known to the Aboriginal people as "White Ghost," while fur traders used the name "La Montaigne de la Grande Traverse." On some early park maps, the designation is "Mount Geikie," while other maps use the name "Fitzhugh." In 1915, any toponymical confusion ended when the name was officially changed in honour of Edith Cavell, a British nurse whose execution during World War I led to a global outcry over the injustice of her sentence.

When looking southeast over the rail line from downtown Jasper, you can see Mount Tekarra, which lies at the north end of the Maligne Range between the Athabasca River Valley and the Maligne River Valley. It was named in 1859 by Dr. James Hector of the Palliser Expedition in honour of his Iroquois guide.

Roche Bonhomme is best known to Jasper locals as "Old Man Mountain" for its face-like profile. Its official name, a loose translation of "Good Fellow," is attributed to George Munro Grant, secretary to Sir Sanford Fleming during an 1872 survey of the Athabasca River Valley. The valley's earliest Métis settlers believed the mountain was a guardian and called it "Grandfather Mountain."

Rising gracefully to the north of the town is Pyramid Mountain, whose name, bestowed by James Hector in 1859, is obvious to all who lay eyes on this symmetrical peak. Its subtle pink colouring comes from iron-rich rock that has been dated at almost one billion years old. Pyramid is the highest point of the Victoria Cross Range, which comprises 16 mountains, seven of which are named for recipients of Canada's highest military honour.

However, on February 15, 1881, CPR officials made the surprising decision to route the rail line through the more southerly Bow Valley and Kicking Horse Pass and leave the Athabasca River Valley to its few resident Métis families.

For one simple Quaker woman, the beauty of the Canadian Rockies lay far off the beaten path. Mary Schäffer dedicated her summers to exploring forgotten regions in the Rockies. It may be surprising to think that a woman in the 1900s was allowed to travel the wild trails of Canada amidst the crude company of packers and guides, and there were likely people who frowned at Schäffer's behaviour. But she did not see how enjoying nature could possibly be equated with indecency, and as a result, she helped to usher in a new era of feminine freedom in a post-Victorian world.

Born Mary Townsend Sharples on October 4, 1861, she grew up in a middle class and well-educated Quaker family from Philadelphia. From a young age, she was encouraged to cultivate her skills in photography and painting. In 1887, 26-year-old Sharples first travelled to the Canadian Rockies along the newly laid CPR with Dr. Charles Schäffer, a friend of Sharples's father, as her chaperone. Although Dr. Schäffer was 23 years older than Sharples, they found kindred spirits in each other, especially when it came to their shared love of natural history. They married two years later, in 1889. The couple spent most of their summers together exploring the Canadian Rockies until Dr. Schäffer passed away unexpectedly in 1903.

After her husband's death, Schäffer entered a new chapter in her life. In honour of her deceased husband, she returned to the Canadian Rockies in 1904. Banff outfitter Tom Wilson recommended Billy Warren, one of his guides, to lead her through the Canadian wilderness. Over the next few summers, she used her husband's botanical studies to write *Alpine Flora of the Canadian Rockies*, which was published in 1907. After reading *Climbs and Explorations in the Canadian Rockies* (1903), by Hugh Stutfield and John Norman Collie, Schäffer became interested in exploring what lay north of the Columbia Icefield.

Returning from a 1907 journey to Brazeau Lake, guides Billy Warren and Sid Unwin led her party to the Kootenay Plains, where their boss, Tom Wilson, had a cabin. While at Kootenay Plains, they were invited to dinner with Wilson's neighbour and fellow outfitter Elliot Barnes. Samson and Leah Beaver and their daughter Frances Louise were also at the dinner. Much of the discussion that night revolved around the North Saskatchewan River Valley, the area from which Schäffer and her party had just returned. When Schäffer spoke of her fascination with the stories she had heard of Chaba Imne, Samson surprised her by saying that not only did he know of the lake but he had visited it as a child with his father. Luckily for Schäffer, Samson remembered the way to the lake and drew her a map. The evening would prove to be momentous for both Schäffer and the history of the Canadian Rockies.

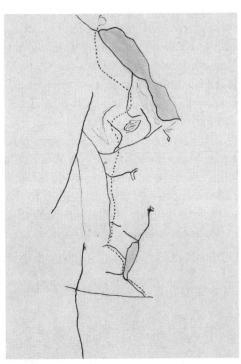

The map drawn by Samson Beaver bore a remarkable likeness to Maligne Lake.

The following summer, in 1908, Schäffer made another attempt to find the lake. Guided again by Warren and Unwin, she was accompanied by her close friend Mary "Mollie" Adams, botanist Stewardson Brown, a cook, and 22 horses. Little did the group know that this would be the trip that would make them part of Jasper National Park's history forever.

From Lake Louise, with Beaver's map in hand, they travelled north over Wilcox Pass to the Sunwapta River and then over Poboktan Pass. Travelling by horse usually made things easier, but in her journal, Schäffer wrote of the great difficulty that they had getting their horses through the densely overgrown trails. Gnarly tree roots tangled themselves around the horses' hooves and made progress extremely slow. The bank of one creek in particular was so bad that Schäffer aptly named it "Tangle Foot."

Regardless of their difficulties, the party eventually reached Maligne Pass. After setting up a camp, Unwin set off, exclaiming, "I'm going to climb something that's high enough to see if that lake's within twenty miles of here, and I'm not coming back until I know!" Then at approximately 10:30 p.m., Unwin appeared through the darkness at camp and shouted, "I've found the lake!" The following morning, the party reached the shore of Chaba Imne. Warren and Unwin set about felling timber to build a raft, which took just one day to build. It was christened HMS *Chaba*, and the entire party paddled out into the heart of the vast body of water known today as Maligne Lake. Schäffer later wrote: " . . . all in our little company agreed, it was the finest view any of us had

Pushing off from the shoreline aboard HMS Chaba, *1908.*

beheld in the Rockies. This was a tremendous assertion, for, of that band of six of us, and each counted his miles of travel through them by thousands. Yet it lay there, for the time being all ours, — those miles and miles of lake, the unnamed peaks rising above us, one following the other, each more beautiful than the last."

By the time Schäffer published *Old Indian Trails* in early 1911, which included a detailed account of her expedition to Maligne Lake, her fame had spread. At the time, both the government and the Grand Trunk Pacific Railway were eager to see Maligne Lake mapped and surveyed so that it could be open to the expected crowds of tourists that would begin arriving by train. Upon the urging of Donaldson B. Dowling of the Geological Survey of Canada (GSC), Schäffer returned to Maligne Lake in the summer of 1911. On this occasion, sponsored by the GTP, she did not travel via the old hunting trails from the south as she had done in 1908 but instead rode the train west from Edmonton to Hinton, or as she described, along the "iron python—an intrusive creature born of an industrial age penetrating deep into once sacred places . . . " Accompanying Schäffer was her sister in-law Caroline Sharples and Caroline's 10-year-old son, Paul.

Of her arrival in Hinton in early June 1911, Schäffer wrote: "Out from the mass of unnumbered nationalities yelled a bona fide bus driver, 'All aboard for Prairie Creek and the Mountain View Hotel!' We saw our tents and blankets and duffle-bag take a flying leap from the baggage van to the waiting mud, and then — O joy! Out of that sea of unknown quantities loomed the familiar face of Jack Otto, our famous old guide from Field, B.C. He was riding a handsome sorrel, and his welcome smile, as he quickly rescued the blankets from the Hinton soil, was worth all the 'Mountain Views' in creation."

From Hinton, Otto guided the Schäffer party west along the Athabasca River past the distinct peak of Roche Miette and the mining town of Pocahontas before setting up camp on the shore of Jasper Lake at the site of Jasper House, which had been abandoned two decades earlier. Rather than using the Maligne Valley to access

Maligne Lake, the government requested that Schäffer survey a trail that had been cut running south from the railway to Buffalo Prairie and then east along Wabasso Creek and up and over the Maligne Range to the north of Curator Mountain. Although snow still covered the trail at higher elevations, Otto guided them to the north shore of Maligne Lake, which they reached on June 19, 1911. Making the journey more difficult was the problem of transporting a rather heavy and cumbersome wooden boat up to the lake. Otto rose to the challenge; he disassembled the boat and tied the planks to the side of his horse. The long planks made it impossible for the horse to navigate its own path, so Jack guided it and used the planks like a rudder to steer.

Maligne Lake was to be Schäffer's home for the next six weeks. And while her cheery description of their camp suggests an easy and idyllic vacation, there was work to be done. Using a compass, Schäffer began surveying the lake. She later wrote, "It did not take more than two days' work for me to realize it was no child's play, or the work a matter of a few days." Mary and her crew worked from north to south, taking measurements to create a survey that was used to create the first official government map of Maligne Lake. As part of her submission to the government, Schäffer suggested names for many of the surrounding geological features, including mounts Warren and Unwin for her guides and Samson and Leah peaks for her Stoney friends. For the peak beside Unwin, Schäffer proposed Mount Charlton, for Harry Ready Charlton, GTP publicity agent. As was the toponymic standard, Schäffer chose to name Maligne Lake for the river it fed. All names were approved by the Geological Survey of Canada in November 1911.

Another aspect to exploration of the Canadian Rockies was mountaineering. Prior to the establishment of Jasper Forest Park in 1907, few of the peaks within the new park boundaries had been climbed, and most of the park's southern half was yet to be explored.

One of the first seasoned mountaineers to venture into the southern end of the park around the Columbia Icefield was a

Jack Otto crossing Shovel Pass in 1911.

Shovel Pass

In the spring of 1911, in anticipation of Mary Schäffer's survey of Maligne Lake, a trail was cut through the Maligne Range by a group of local men that included Closson and Bruce Otto. When the workers reached a snow-covered pass below Curator Mountain, they fashioned shovels from nearby spruce trees. The route used by Schäffer is crossed by today's Skyline Trail, and the pass is known as Shovel Pass, which is also the name of a backcountry lodge along the trail. The original crude wooden shovels can be viewed at the Jasper-Yellowhead Museum.

the wooden shovels

Billy Warren (right)

Mount Warren

One of the highest mountains in the Maligne Lake area is the 3,362-metre (11,030-foot) Mount Warren, at its remote south end. William "Billy" Warren guided Mary Schäffer throughout the Canadian Rockies, and their travels took them to the shore of Maligne Lake in 1908. When Schäffer first saw the mountain upon which she bestowed her guide's name, she described it as "massive and dignified"—two qualities that she associated with Warren's kind and generous nature.

Warren, like many of the earliest guides in the Canadian Rockies, was originally from England. He was born at Harlow, Essex, in 1880. In 1899, he joined the Imperial Yeomanry and served throughout the duration of the Boer Wars. Warren then crossed the Atlantic Ocean in search of adventure in the wilds of western Canada. Arriving in Banff in 1903, he found employment with outfitter Tom Wilson. After one season as a wrangler, he was promoted to the position of guide. Warren's first client was Schäffer, and their relationship evolved into marriage in June 1915.

By 1919, Warren foresaw automobiles as the future of mountain travel. He opened a garage on Banff's main street and then converted an old livery into Rocky Mountain Tours & Transport (now home to Banff's famous Grizzly House restaurant). Although he remains best known for his historic link to Maligne Lake, Warren's career shift from trail guide to businessman proved to be a wise one, and he sealed his place as one of Banff's most successful businessmen.

German professor, Jean Habel; he reached the headwaters of the Athabasca River in 1901, and travelled up the Chaba River to the Chaba Glacier. Habel also recorded the existence of Mount Columbia, which he was unable to climb because of poor weather. He organized a trip with outfitter Tom Wilson to climb Columbia the following summer, but passed away early in 1902. Habel Creek, near the Columbia Icefield, and Mount Habel, on the Continental Divide, were named in his honour.

Approximately 80 years earlier, in 1827, Scottish botanist David Douglas (for whom the Douglas fir tree was named) had spotted two distant mountains as his party rested near Athabasca Pass. Douglas's diary entry from the expedition stated:

Being well rested by one o'clock, I set out with the view of ascending what seemed to be the highest peak on the N. Its height does not appear to be less than 16,000 or 17,000 feet above the level of the sea. After passing over the lower ridge, I came to about 12,000 feet of by far the most difficult and fatiguing walking I ever experienced . . . The view from the summit is of too awful a cast to afford pleasure. Nothing can be seen in every direction except mountains towering above each other, rugged beyond description. The majestic but terrible avalanches, hurling themselves from the more exposed southerly rocks, produced a crash and groaned through the distant valleys with a sound only equalled by that of an earthquake . . . This peak, the highest yet known in the Northern Continent of America, I felt a sincere pleasure in naming "Mount Brown," in honour of R. Brown, Esq., the illustrious botanist. A little to the southward is one nearly of the same height . . . named "Mount Hooker," in honour of my early patron, the professor of Botany in the University of Glasgow. This mountain I was not able to climb.

By the early 1890s, Douglas's diary entry had mountaineers obsessed with locating the two legendary mountains, but no one could find them.

During the last decade of the 1800s, Arthur P. Coleman, Hugh Stutfield, and John Norman Collie were dedicated to climbing where no others had climbed before. Canadian-born Coleman, in particular, was obsessed with locating Douglas's fabled peaks. In 1893, 66 years after Douglas reached Athabasca Pass and after three summers of fruitless searching, Coleman finally reached Committee's Punchbowl (the previous year Coleman had mistaken Fortress Lake for Committee's Punchbowl), which had been named by Sir George Simpson in 1824. He was disappointed to discover that the legendary body of water was more like a pond than a lake. But for Coleman, the greatest disappointment was yet to come. As he scanned the horizon from the point at which Douglas had reported the two distinct peaks, he could not find any mountains that would appear to do Douglas's description justice. The only two mountains that could possibly be Hooker and Brown were most definitely not "towering" or "the highest yet known in the Northern Continent of America." Coleman's disappointment over his discovery of Douglas's miscalculation was made obvious in his own journal; he recorded,

We got the saddles off the ponies and pitched the tent beside the Punch Bowl silently. We had reached our point after six weeks of toil and anxiety, after three summers of effort, and we did not even raise a cheer. Mount Brown and Hooker were frauds, and we were disgusted at having been humbugged by them. Personally, I found some solace for the disappointment as I hobbled round camp, in thought that if I could do no climbing much, for there was no glory to be got in climbing Mount Brown. We had expected to row our canvas boat round the lake on the summit, an occupation that would have suited me, since it did not demand legs; but the Punch Bowl was too small a pool to make it worthwhile, and the boat remained in its pack cover of green canvas. We stayed five days in our camp by the Punch Bowl. While Stewart and my brother explored the surroundings, Frank kept an eye on the ponies, and I loafed about camp . . . "

Five years later, in 1898, a discovery worthy of Douglas's infamous description was made by Collie, who had previously climbed in the European Alps and the Himalayas, and Herman

Woolley, an ex-boxer who did not begin climbing until the age of 40. Led by legendary Banff guide "Wild" Bill Peyto as an outfitter, the men travelled north from Banff to the north fork of the North Saskatchewan River via Pipestone Pass. Using Sunwapta Pass as a base camp, Collie and Woolley set off to reach the summit of Mount Athabasca, which had been recorded two years earlier by Walter Wilcox. When the two men summited the peak, they were afforded sweeping views of the Columbia Icefield, one of the most magnificent natural features of the Canadian Rockies. In the published account *Climbs and Explorations of the Canadian Rockies*, Collie describes the view from the top of Mount Athabasca as "a new world . . . to the westward stretched a vast icefield probably never before seen by human eye, and surrounded by entirely unknown, unnamed, and unclimbed peaks. From its vast expanse of snows the Saskatchewan glacier takes its rise and it also supplies the headwaters of the Athabasca; while far away to the west, bending over those unknown valleys . . . to finally melt and flow down more than one channel into the Columbia River, and thence to the Pacific Ocean." In reaching the peak of Mount Athabasca, Collie and Woolley became the first to record another of Jasper National Park's most spectacular landmarks—Mount Alberta.

4 Railway

n 1869, the Union Pacific Railroad completed a transcontinental railway across what is now the United States, and on November 7, 1885, the CPR completed its own line; it passed through Banff and crossed the Continental Divide at Kicking Horse Pass. Although Sir Sandford Fleming of the Canadian Pacific Survey had visited the Athabasca River Valley as early as the 1870s, the construction of the CPR track along a more southerly route had left what is now Jasper National Park quiet for almost three decades. This would change shortly after the turn of the new century, however.

Although the CPR dominated the Canadian railroad industry in the late 1800s, by the turn of the new century two companies were challenging its monopoly. Established in 1899, the Canadian Northern Railway (CNoR) was based in Manitoba and primarily operated branch lines from the CPR. The company was operated by business partners William Mackenzie and Donald Mann, who had begun their careers with the CPR. After achieving success, the CNoR expanded beyond the prairies; it began operating steamships on the Great Lakes and built a rail line between Toronto and Montreal.

Headquartered in London, England, the Grand Trunk Railway (GTR) was a polished and high-profile company formed in 1852 to build a rail line between Toronto and Montreal. By 1900, its lines extended throughout the eastern provinces and New England. Representing the company to the Canadian government were two savvy businessmen, Charles Rivers-Wilson and Charles Melville Hays. Both Rivers-Wilson and Hays were masters in the art of lobbying.

By 1900, the men representing both the GTR and the CNoR had become familiar faces in Ottawa and were well known for their lobbying attempts. Both companies were desperate for government support in the form of funding and land. The linchpin in these negotiations was Prime Minister Wilfred Laurier, who had come into power in July, 1896. The opposition party ensured that Canadians were aware of Laurier's long-standing friendship with Rivers-Wilson and took every opportunity to expose Laurier's

A railway construction crew in the Athabasca River Valley.

intention to leave the Canadian taxpayer with the bill. Laurier, on the other hand, was desperate to avoid leaving a second-rate, patchwork railroad as his legacy.

In 1903, Laurier passed legislation aimed at creating a second transcontinental rail line, which would link Winnipeg with Prince Rupert, on the Pacific Ocean. Although both the GTR and the CNoR signed agreements with the government, they did so based on a variety of conditions. Part of the GTR agreement stated that they would create a western Canadian subsidiary (Grand Trunk Pacific, or GTP) as a way of ensuring that profits would stay within Canada. Most importantly, the agreement stated that the CNoR and GTR would share the Yellowhead Pass. The race to the Yellowhead Pass had begun.

By 1905, the CNoR line had reached Edmonton, which had been incorporated as a city the year before, when its population was little more than 8,300. When the CNoR line was completed to Edmonton, the GTP line barely extended west of Winnipeg. In a notorious attempt to get ahead, the GTP filed plans that outlined its intent to survey through Peace River country before heading for the mountains, and so the CNoR, with a false sense of their lead, constructed a number of branch lines from Edmonton.

Railway construction during the early 1900s was usually done on a contract basis. One of the best-known contracting companies at the time was Foley, Welch and Stewart, which built track for major railway companies across North America, including the GTP, which was well ahead of the CNoR when it came to reaching the Yellowhead Pass. The contracting company set up construction camps, hired its own workers, and oversaw the safety of workers. Railway construction teams consisted of up to 120 labourers, many of whom were newly arrived immigrants. The teams were further divided into more specialized groups that would handle specific stages of construction: surveying, clearing, building culverts, building bridges, grading, and track-laying.

The Importance of Coal

Coal is North America's most common fossil fuel and was mined within what is now Jasper National Park between 1910 and 1921, as well as immediately east of the park in what is known as the Coal Branch. Alberta contains 70 percent of Canada's known coal resources, much of it low in sulphur, meaning it burns cleanly and efficiently. Large deposits were mined as early as 1882 in Lethbridge, with mines opening the following year in Canmore and Edmonton. By the onset of World War I, coal mining had developed into a major industry within Alberta. Coal was used to heat homes and provide fuel for steam locomotives, making discoveries along rail lines especially important.

Coal production throughout Alberta jumped from 244,420 tons in the late 1890s to over three million tons by 1913 and by 1914, coal mining was one of Alberta's primary industries. That year, coal mining in Alberta comprised nearly 30 percent of Canada's total coal production; 3.56 million tons of coal were produced and 8,000 people were employed.

The declaration of World War I on August 14, 1914, had an immediate and powerful effect on economies around the world, including Alberta's. Alberta coal mines saw a substantial jump in production from 1.73 million tons in 1911 to 4.64 million tons by 1916, due to the war. The bulk of the wartime coal went to the CPR, flourmills, and farmers across Canada. Coal mines in Lethbridge, Canmore, Edmonton, Drumheller, and the Crowsnest Pass saw increased production, and new coal fields were opened, including through the Coal Branch, an area south of Hinton bordering the eastern boundary of Jasper National Park. By the 1920s, mining communities along the Coal Branch included Cadomin, Robb, Mercoal,

The survey crew was the lead crew and worked well in advance of the other groups. They marked out the route by hammering stakes into the ground while also surveying the best locations for railway stations, train yards, and even hotels. They needed to work quickly to stay ahead of rail line construction. After the surveyors had completed their work east from Edson, Foley, Welch and Stewart employed labourers to build a tote road paralleling the planned route of the rail line. The terrain west of Edson was particularly rough, with bridges built across creeks and ferries set up to cross wider rivers. Camps were established approximately every three kilometres along the tote road. Although lumber from felled trees was used to construct buildings, the camps were generally filled

Lovett, Luscar, and Mountain Park, all of which were linked to the GTP by a branch line that spurred south from Edson.

As diesel began to replace coal as a locomotive fuel after World War II, the mines began closing and the towns were slowly abandoned. Today, Cadomin and Robb have a combined population of around 250 while the other Coal Branch communities have slid into oblivion.

Coal mining even took place in what is now Jasper National Park.

Many railway labourers were migrant workers, who carried all their possessions with them.

with canvas tents, including a bunkhouse, cookhouse, a general store, and storage areas. Some of the official construction camps expanded over time and were the nucleus of towns that remain in place today. Others were decommissioned and dismantled when construction had been completed.

Once the tote road had been completed, the remaining crews were staggered along the surveyed route and usually worked within 10 kilometres of each other. The first crew to follow the new tote road was assigned to clear the way of forest, brush, and deadfall. Any timber that was of value was set aside; the rest was burned. Following the clearing crew was the culvert crew. These men were responsible for constructing the rail bed and the drainage channels. After the rail beds and culverts were constructed, the bridge crew constructed crude trestles over rivers, canyons, and creeks. A grading crew followed the bridge builders. This crew ensured that the rail bed was level and properly graded. The final phase of rail line construction was track-laying. A flatbed rail car was rigged with a towering wooden frame for laying track. It crept slowly forward at the railhead with a conveyor-type system that moved wooden ties and steel rails to the front of the frame. From here, the ties and rails were manually moved into place and properly secured by workers.

As soon as track was laid, steam trains began hauling freight west from Edmonton to the construction camps; these trains took over from the freighters, who had preceded the track. Freighters subcontracted by Foley, Welch and Stewart hauled supplies ahead of the construction crews. To the supply tents located along the way, the freighters transported everything from timber (for building bridges and ties) to dynamite (for blasting rock) to food (like flour, pork, bacon, and beans).

Like a giant game of follow-the-leader, the various crews made their way from Edmonton to Edson and from Edson towards the mountains. Between Edson and the mountains, there was mud as far as the eye could see. The men soon discovered that this was no ordinary mud: it was muskeg—thick, sticky and seemingly impossible to navigate. Without any road to follow, the surveyors tried wearing their snowshoes in the middle of July just to avoid getting stuck. Luckily, the snowshoes did the trick, and slowly but surely, the surveyors made their way across the gumbo. It took the survey crew approximately two months to cross the muskeg and reach Roche Miette—a natural gateway to the Canadian Rockies.

While camped near the mouth of the Fiddle River (near the present day East Park Gate), the GTP survey crew became aware of a distinctive rotten-egg-like smell. Following the smell to its source up the Fiddle River Valley, they came across pools of hot, mineral-rich water. It would have been obvious to the railway workers that they weren't the first people to reach the hot springs—as the water was dammed by boulders strung across the creek. It is not known who discovered the springs, but the site was known to the fur trade community around Jasper House and by the time the railway workers reached them, there was a rough trail leading up the Fiddle River Valley from the Athabasca River. As early as 1839, Métis fur traders had contained the water into pools for bathing, but it is assumed by historians that the site was previously visited by Aboriginal people.

By the time surveyors with GTP reached Roche Miette, coal seams at its eastern base had been claimed by two prospectors, Frank Villeneuve and Alfred Lamoreau, who had made the discovery in 1908. By the time the GTP reached Roche Miette in

Disaster Point

The original trail into the Athabasca River Valley from the east used by fur traders ran along the east side the Athabasca River. Approximately 40 kilometres northeast of present day Jasper, where the lower slopes of Roche Miette once jutted into the river, travellers were forced to either cross the rushing water or make a dangerous climb up and over a steep ridge; both options often led to disaster. During construction of the GTP railway, dynamite and heavy machinery were used to clear a route around the base of the mountain, but the original name remains to this day.

late 1910, coal was being mined by Jasper Park Collieries at what had become known as Pocahontas.

On September 14, 1907, Jasper Forest Park was established (although it was often referred to as a national park prior to

Pocahontas

Soon after submitting a claim for the seam of coal they had discovered at the base of Roche Miette, Frank Villeneuve and Alfred Lamoreau found investors who bought out their claims and formed Jasper Park Collieries. The company named the property Pocahontas after a successful coalfield in Virginia. The first railcar of coal was loaded in September 1911, and by the following spring, over 40,000 tons of coal had been mined, most of which was used for fuelling GTP trains. By 1912, the GTP had completed construction of a railway station at Pocahontas, and in 1913, a second mine, the Miette, was opened at the base of Bedson Ridge on the west side of the Athabasca River.

As the mines expanded, Jasper Park Collieries surveyed a townsite, which was spread across two natural benches linked by a steep flight of stairs. At its peak, Pocahontas had 250 residents (many were European immigrants), a post office, a church, a school, a mine

the post office at Pocahontas

manager's house, and a cemetery. By 1918, after two miners had died, labour unrest was widespread throughout the province's mining communities, and the company's lack of safety practices had come to the attention of the government mine inspectors. Labour unrest coupled with financial problems led to the mine's closure in 1921. Most of the town and the mining infrastructure was removed soon after.

Today, a paved interpretive trail leads through the abandoned townsite. It passes by the site of mine manager's house, concrete foundations, various other ruins, and an abandoned rail car. The trail begins approximately 45 kilometres north of the town of Jasper at a parking area just off Highway 16 along the road to Miette Hot Springs.

Looking north across the Pocahontas mine to the Athabasca River.

The remains of Swift's waterwheel.

the 1930 National Parks Act being passed). Initially, the park was managed by the deputy minister of the Department of the Interior. The new park encompassed 12,950 square kilometres of mountainous wilderness; there were no roads and existing trails were from the fur-trading era.

In 1909, John W. McLaggan, acting superintendent of the new park, approached the valley's seven recorded homesteaders and cajoled them to leave the valley with offers of financial compensation; he anticipated that they would all leave by the time the rail line was completed, but he was not prepared for a stubborn obstacle—Lewis Swift.

Born on February 24, 1854, in Berlin, Ohio, Swift was a young man when he headed east to Buffalo, New York, in search of work. He then travelled west to South Dakota, where he gained a reputation as a daring stagecoach driver on the route between Bismarck and Deadwood. In the early 1890s, Swift headed to Canada, lured by the promise of a fortune on the goldfields. Although he made a couple of mine claims in southern British Columbia, he failed to make any worthwhile amounts of money.

Around 1892, Swift reached the Athabasca River and settled into the abandoned buildings of Jasper House, and established a small vegetable garden. On one of his trips to Edmonton for supplies, Swift met Suzette Chalifoux, with whom he established a farm near the base of The Palisade, a sheer cliff that rises from the floor of the Athabasca River Valley. Here, Swift and Chalifoux built a long, low, log cabin and surrounded themselves with livestock,

Suzette Swift

Suzette Swift

Suzette Chalifoux was born in St. Albert, a Métis settlement northwest of Edmonton, on May 20, 1866. Chalifoux's parents were from Lac Ste. Anne. She attended school at a convent located in St. Albert. The convent was run by the Grey Nuns and also served as an orphanage. The young girls of St. Albert learned how to cook, sew, iron, and grow gardens with the help of the older women and the nuns. The intensive training in domestic tasks was offered so that the young girls could get jobs in the city of Edmonton as housemaids.

Chalifoux's first position upon leaving the convent was as a maid in the house of John Norris, of Edmonton. The Norrises were a well-established and well-to-do family. Chalifoux worked for them until the death of Norris's wife, Marie Pelletier. Chalifoux then went to live with some family friends, the Wylies, who lived outside of Edmonton. It was during her time here that she met her future husband, Lewis Swift, with whom she raised a family on a homestead east of present-day Jasper.

In 1935, Suzette and Lewis moved into a house on Patricia Street in the developing town of Jasper and quickly became neighbourhood favourites. Suzette was known for bestowing handmade, beaded moccasins on newly born babies in town. Suzette lived until the age of 80 and died on November 14, 1946. She is buried, along with her children and husband, in the Jasper Cemetery.

including chickens, cows, and horses. Swift diverted water from a creek to a waterwheel used to grind grain into flour and meal. The couple also established a vegetable garden and traded produce with local Métis families. The couple were married on September 3, 1897, in Edmonton. Born in 1899, Charlotte (Lottie) was their first child together; she was followed by Ida Edith (1901), Dean Lewis (1902), James Willis (1904), James William (1907), and John Sidney (1911). At just age two, the elder James was fatally shot by Chalifoux's 11-year-old son Albert, whom she had borne prior to her marriage to Lewis.

When GTP surveyors reached Swift's property in the summer of 1909, he brandished a loaded rifle and held the men at bay until they agreed to reroute the railway line around his property. He argued that he had applied for title to his land before the establishment of Jasper Forest Park. Swift was the only Athabasca River Valley homesteader to decline the government offer, despite the fact that McLaggan explained to him that there was to be no privately owned land within the boundaries of the park. His refusal was not in protest of the government's action, nor was it

Laying the rail line through the Athabasca River Valley.

in protest of the injustice that had been done to his neighbours who had accepted; instead, he assumed that one of the railway companies making their way through the valley might be willing to pay more than what the government was offering. Eventually, Swift was granted full ownership of 158 acres.

Although there is no written proof, it has been said that Swift later negotiated directly with Charles Melville Hays, who in 1905 had been appointed president of the GTP, and that their discussions led to a joint real estate venture. Swift agreed to offer up a portion of his property to be surveyed and subdivided into lots for a resort that would be named in his honour—Swiftholm. Advertisements were placed in Edmonton newspapers boasting of a "beautifully laid out summer resort." Unfortunately for Swift, the GTP began to face financial problems in the lead up to World War I, and the plan never went any further than a survey. Any agreement was also complicated by the fact that on April 14, 1912, Hays perished aboard the RMS *Titanic* while returning to Canada from a company meeting in London, England, at which a business plan for the revival of GTP fortunes had been formulated.

While Swift stood up to the government demands, the Métis families who had lived in the valley for generations had no choice but to accept the compensation offered. In 1910, Ewan Moberly and his family left the Athabasca River Valley and made the long trek to Victor Lake (near Grande Cache); he cut trail as he led his family and 200 head of cattle north from the land he had known his entire life. Also moving north to Victor Lake were Moberly's grown sons, Adolphus and William, and their families. That same year, John Moberly, his wife Marie Joachim, and their seven children moved east to Prairie Creek, near Hinton. According to government documents, Adam Joachim was paid $1,200 for his property, which included two cabins, three acres of cultivated land, stables, and fencing. At the time, Adam was married to Fresnine Moberly, daughter of Ewan Moberly, and they had four children (Adam would go on to father another 13 children). In 1910, Adam and his family also moved north to Victor Lake. He continued to trap and hunt, and he worked as a guide in what is now Willmore Wilderness Park and as a horse packer for Curly Phillips. His memory was honoured by the naming of Mount Adam Joachim. Isadore Findlay and his wife Philomene Karakonti also moved to the Grande Cache area, where their son Deome became a well-respected outfitter.

Today, the descendents of Athabasca River Valley Métis who relocated to the Grande Cache and Hinton areas are known as "Aseniwuche Winewak," a Cree term that translates as "Rocky Mountain People." The best place to soak up the history of Métis life in the Athabasca River Valley is at the site of the Ewan Moberly homestead. Along the Celestine Lake Road, an interpretive trail winds past two log cabins to the grave of Suzanne Karakonti, who remained in the valley raising her two sons John and Ewan after their father, Henry Moberly, left in 1861. The remains of John Moberly's homestead are situated along the Overlander Trail, a two-hour walk north of the lower end of Maligne Canyon.

By 1911, Swift was the lone homesteader of Jasper Forest Park. Travellers who stopped at Swift's home continued to be treated well; they enjoyed good company and, if they were lucky, a swig of moonshine from Swift's little brown jug. Explorer and mountaineer Arthur P. Coleman made the following observations in his book *The Canadian Rockies: New and Old Trails*: "Swift is a most interesting character, a white man of some energy and resource who married a woman of the country, an Iroquois half-breed, many years ago, and had now a brood of wholesome-looking children playing about his log house. He had fenced and ploughed some fields, from which wheat and oats and barley had just been harvested, and had built a watermill on the stream that irrigated his farm to grind his wheat into flour, somewhat brown in colour, but making good bread; so that, except for sugar, tea and tobacco, he was as nearly independent as a man can be."

Swift eventually sold his homestead in 1935—not to the government, who felt the asking price of $6000 was too high, but to Arnold Charles Wilby, a visitor from England who eventually

Railway engineer Vincent Hope in what was typical engineer tent accommodation at the construction camps.

established a ranch-style accommodation known as Pyramid Mountain Lodge. Upon Wilby's death in 1945, the property was sold to Gordon Bried, who continued to operate the lodge (although the name was changed to Palisades Motel); it remained the only privately owned land within a Canadian national park until the government was finally able to purchase the land in 1962. Today, many of the buildings from the Wilby era remain and the site is used as an outdoor education facility by Parks Canada.

After selling their homestead to Wilby in 1935, the Swifts moved into town, living out their remaining years in a house on Patricia Street. Lewis Swift died on 24 March, 1940, and is buried in the Jasper cemetery.

In 1911, four years after Jasper Forest Park was established and before the rail line was completed, the Department of the Interior created the Dominion Parks Branch; James Bernard Harkin was appointed as commissioner. Harkin believed that a park should not be maintained merely for its wilderness; he wrote that a park should be maintained so that "every citizen of Canada may satisfy his soul-craving for nature and nature's beauty; that he may

Lewis Swift in his later years.

absorb the energy and power of the sunshine and the fresh air; that nature's smiles may be reflected into him and that he may sing with the wind and laugh with mountain torrents."

Jasper's first Game and Fire Guardian was Lewis Swift, who was appointed in January 1910 and served through to August of that same year. The government knew firsthand of Swift's tenacity through ongoing negotiations regarding his Athabasca River Valley homestead, and they needed someone for the position who knew the area. Swift worked for the government for less than one year, but his diary reads like a who's who of the Athabasca River Valley. He documented the names of the park's earliest guides, including John Yates and Fred Stephens; he noted his encounters with GTP surveyors, wrote of the destruction of early landmarks such as Jasper House, and, perhaps most importantly, recorded the day when he had to place padlocks on the empty homesteads of his Métis neighbours who had been forced to move out of the new park.

Harkin's vision for parks such as Jasper required manpower, so to ensure that his ideals were met and maintained, Alex McDougall was hired in 1912 as Jasper's first official chief warden. Records show that he was assisted in his duties by Richard (Dick) Langford, who would replace McDougall as chief park warden after World War I; Jimmie Rootes, who married Jasper's first school teacher, Miss Lillian Taylor; and George Busby, who was assigned to the coal-mining settlement of Pocahontas.

McDougall and his wardens were more like a labour crew than guardians of the wild. They cut many of the park's first official trails. Annual reports for the period proudly tell of new trails to Caledonia Lake (part of today's Saturday Night Lake Circuit) and Jasper Lake, trails from the Athabasca River up into Maligne Canyon, and trails between Medicine Lake and the Interlaken Railway Station, which was beside Edna Lake near Pocahontas.

After World War I, returning Canadian soldiers were offered jobs as park wardens across the country. These men had left their jobs and their families to fight for their country, and when they returned, they were unemployed and in some cases unemployable. Returned servicemen hired to work in Jasper Forest Park included Dick Langford, who was appointed chief warden, Percy Goodair, Ed McDonald, George Camp, Frank Bryant, and Herb Davies. The new wardens were given uniforms that had a familiar military style, but instead of hard helmets, they wore soft-brimmed Stetsons and instead of combat fatigues, riding breeches. Decorated veterans were permitted to wear their ribbons alongside their warden badges. The fully outfitted wardens were no longer confused with tourists or outfitters. After days or even weeks patrolling the park, they were expected to check in with the chief warden to submit their diaries and replenish supplies. When a warden failed to show up in town, it usually meant something was wrong.

At the same time that Métis families were leaving the valley, both the GTP and the CNoR were constructing their own rail lines west from Edmonton, although the GTP railhead was well

The GTP and CNoR built parallel rail lines between Edmonton and the Athabasca River Valley.

ahead of their competition. The tracks of the two companies ran so close together in some places that, according to local lore, you could shake hands with passengers on the other train. Having rival companies within such close proximity caused animosity among employees. Those employed by the GTP referred to the Canadian Northerners' as "wooden axels," in reference to the outdated tools they used, and employees of the CNoR called those who worked for the GTP "leaky roofs," a jab at the cash-strapped company's inability to purchase new boxcars.

In August 1911, the GTP established a divisional point on a low plateau above the confluence of the Athabasca and Miette rivers; it was known as Mile 112, for the distance as measured from Wolf Creek, a major railway construction camp east of present day Edson. When construction crews moved on, a few people remained and a small settlement began to form. It was named Fitzhugh, for Earl Hopkins Fitzhugh, a vice-president of the GTR.

After the GTP railway station was completed at Mile 112 in 1912, it too was named for Fitzhugh. The station was prominently located along the main, and only, road through town (in approximately the same location as the current Jasper Railway Station). It had a standard station-type design used by the GTP.

The GTP railway station at Fitzhugh was completed in 1912.

This photo of the GTP railway station was taken after the settlement had been renamed Jasper.

The railway construction camp at the Yellowhead Pass came to be known as Summit City.

It cost $6,314 to build and although it looked comfortable from the outside, the sparsely constructed interior had a reputation for being drafty.

When a disgruntled Fitzhugh resigned from the GTR after disagreements with his fellow vice presidents following the death of Hays, he filed a lawsuit against his former employer. After lengthy and contentious court proceedings, the parent company of the GTP, the GTR removed all references to Fitzhugh from their files and went so far as to encourage the government to rename the settlement that had become known as Fitzhugh. The new name chosen, Jasper, a tribute to Jasper Haws, the fur trader who had manned the lonely Athabasca River Valley post almost a century before, was made official on June 1, 1913.

Construction of the CNoR rail line was around 10 months behind the GTP. The two lines owned by competing companies ran parallel to each other all the way from Edmonton and over the Yellowhead Pass. In 1913, the CNoR established their divisional point on the west side of Yellowhead Pass at what became known as Lucerne. By 1915, the CNoR had also completed a railway station in Jasper; it was one kilometre west of the GTP station (the site is marked by an interpretive panel along the Discovery Trail). Designed by Winnipeg architect Ralph Benjamin Pratt, it was similar to many other CNoR stations of the era with its high-hipped roof and gabled dormers. The fieldstone exterior featured many large windows that faced the tracks so passengers could watch for their train while sitting inside. When the two railway companies were amalgamated, the GTP station was kept in service and the CNoR station was converted to a bunkhouse for railway employees. When Lou Purcell, a railway engineer, was living in the bunkhouse, he put up a sign that read "Sleepy Hollow." Eventually, in 1974, the CNoR station was demolished.

During World War I, the Canadian government sent resources such as steel to Europe to help with the war effort. The twin tracks running through Jasper were deemed superfluous, and it was decided that one line was needed. The GTP track was chosen over the CNoR track to be sent overseas as it had a heavier gauge and was made of better quality steel, but as the GTP was considered to have the superior rail bed along much of the route, the lighter

Completed in 1915, the CNoR station was one kilometre was of the present day Jasper Railway Station.

gauge CNoR track was moved, and by 1917 only one rail line remained.

By the end of World War I, both railway companies were facing financial difficulties. In an attempt to prevent a complete collapse of Canada's railway industry, the government began buying up struggling railway companies, including the CNoR in September, 1918, and the GTP in July, 1920. By 1922, these two companies along with others across Canada were amalgamated into the Canadian National Railway (CNR). The first president of the CNR after 1922 was the charismatic Sir Henry Thornton. He focused on ensuring rail travel was passenger friendly, encouraged immigrants to settle in rural areas along the CNR lines, and he marketed railway towns as tourist destinations. Jasper, in particular, was advertised as a great wilderness escape.

The CNoR divisional point at Lucerne was abandoned in 1924 and many of its 350 residents moved to Jasper. Many of the

Silk Trains

Between 1925 and 1932, trains would regularly pass through Jasper carrying shipments of raw silk used to make luxury clothing. With cargo that deteriorated rapidly and that was worth several millions of dollars, speed and safety were priorities. After a sea voyage from Asia, the silk was loaded onto trains in Vancouver; then it was transported by rail to New York's National Silk Exchange. The silk was carried in sealed baggage cars lined with paper to protect it from soot and dampness. Each silk train was accompanied by armed guards and given priority over other trains, including those for passengers. Reaching speeds of up to 140 kilometres per hour, the silk trains travelled across Canada faster than any trains before them. When they stopped at divisional points like Jasper to change crews or locomotives, the processes were expedited. When they crossed the border into the United States, customs protocols were often set aside.

Before Henry Thornton was put in charge of the CNR in 1922, the CPR had had a monopoly on silk transportation in Canada. However, as a result of Thornton's lobbying, the CNR received part of the business. Between 1925, when the first CNR silk train left Vancouver, and 1932, by which time man-made fibres were replacing silk, approximately 100 of the legendary silk trains passed through Jasper.

Locomotive 6060 was on display in Jasper until 1973.

Lucerne houses were also relocated, including to 120 Connaught Drive, which is the only remaining Lucerne home in Jasper.

After World War II, advancements were made in the world of locomotive engines. The CNR replaced the slow, boxy black engines used in the early part of the last century with larger, stronger, and faster engines. These sleek locomotives were known as "Bullet Nose Bettys" for the shape of the smoke box door cover. The Bettys also marked the end of an era; automobiles became more affordable and changed the way people travelled, which brought a close to the golden age of rail travel to Jasper. A couple of Bettys are still used for steam train excursions around Canada, including locomotive 6060, which was restored by local railroad enthusiast Harry Home; it was on display in Jasper until 1973 and is now used by Alberta Prairie Railway Excursions in Stettler, Alberta, for day trips through the region.

The 6060 once displayed in Jasper has since been replaced by imposing, midnight-black locomotive 6015, a Mountain Type steam engine which was used between 1923 and 1955.

5 Early Tourism

In the early part of the 1900s, visitors from around the world were travelling aboard Canadian Pacific Railway trains to Banff National Park. They would stay at the newly built mountain resort hotels, often for the entire summer, and explore the wilderness, climb mountains, and kill big game for trophies. Generally, this new breed of tourists was wealthy and more than happy to pay well for guiding and outfitting services. It was into this environment that, by the time the first passenger trains began rolling into Fitzhugh in 1912, a number of guides and outfitters had already established businesses in anticipation of a similar tourism boom.

The Moberly brothers, born in the Athabasca River Valley, were among the earliest guides actually based in Jasper Forest Park. Only a handful of guides based their outfitting businesses within the park (most others worked between Jasper and Banff) and those who did—the Moberlys, the Brewsters, the Hargreaves, the Ottos, and Curly Phillips—played an important role in Jasper's development as a tourist destination. They combined a love of adventure with a flair for business, sensing the park's potential as an opportunity to do business with those who were looking for adventure in the Canadian Rockies.

One of Jasper's best-known outfitters was Frederick Archibald Brewster, who was born in Kildonan, Manitoba, in 1884. His parents, John and Isabella Brewster, moved west from Manitoba in 1888 and established a dairy to provide milk for the Banff Springs Hotel. After earning an engineering degree from Queen's University in Ontario, Fred and his younger brother, Jack, arrived in the Athabasca River valley in the spring of 1911. After spending a year working as a freighter on the GTP rail line, which was being constructed through the valley, the two brothers had enough money to start their own guiding business. Along with their brother-in-law, Phil Moore, Fred and Jack established Brewster and Moore's in 1912. Fred was a voracious reader of early literature regarding the Canadian Rockies, which made him a favourite with scientific expeditions looking for knowledgeable locals; he also guided big game hunters and wealthy tourists who arrived on the newly

Fred Brewster served with distinction in World War I.

Azalea Adams

Azalea Adams grew up in New York during the early years of the last century and enjoyed a childhood of wealth and privilege. In the early 1920s, she was swept off her feet by Jasper entrepreneur Fred Brewster, who had recently returned from World War I and was visiting New York on business. Disenfranchised with New York's high society, she returned to Jasper with Brewster in 1924. According to an article in a 1926 edition of *Canadian National Railway*

Magazine, the young socialite adapted well to the remote Canadian Rockies—Brewster built her an impressive log home in Jasper, showed her how to cook on the trail, and taught her wilderness survival skills.

In 1928, however, in her mid-30s and after living in Jasper for only a few years, Adams was diagnosed with a

Azalea is buried in the Jasper cemetery.

bipolar disorder. It was an era when mental disorders and depression were not widely discussed, so little is known about her later years except that she passed away in 1961 at a psychiatric hospital in Quebec. Brewster brought her body back to Jasper so she could be buried in Jasper Cemetery. The couple did not have any children, and Brewster never remarried.

completed railway. During this time, he visited Maligne Lake a number of times and travelled along a rough trail running up the Rocky River and through the Colin Range via Jacques Lake.

Before the onset of World War I, Fred Brewster and a crew of local men were contracted by the government to clear a wagon road up the Maligne Valley as far as Medicine Lake. It ran along the base of Old Fort Point and between Lakes Edith and Annette before switchbacking up to the top of Maligne Canyon.

Brewster subsequently established tent camps at the south end of Medicine Lake and the north end of Maligne Lake. Guests travelled by horseback from the Athabasca River Valley up the Maligne Valley on the wagon road and then along Medicine Lake to a junction with an old trail that led down from Jacques

Lake. Arriving at the south end of Medicine Lake, tourists were accommodated in primitive tent cabins, which comprised a planked floor and a wooden frame covered with canvas. Two tents were set up for sleeping and a third for dining. From Medicine Lake, it was a full day's horseback ride to Maligne Lake, where a similar cluster of tent cabins overlooked the north end of the lake. The first guests—Josephine Rathbone, a well-travelled librarian from New York, and a young man from the Curtis Publishing Company and his wife—arrived at Brewster's Maligne Lake camp in 1914. At this time, the camp hosted a maximum of four guests at any one time, plus two camp attendants. The raft left behind by Schäffer in 1911 was used to take guests out onto the lake.

Competing with the Brewster brothers was another set of siblings—Jack, Closson, and Bruce Otto. The Ottos had previously operated outfitting businesses along the CPR line in Field and Golden. The eldest of the Otto brothers, Jack, had been the first to arrive in the Canadian Rockies, moving west from the family home in Ontario around 1895. By the time Jack was joined by his teenaged brothers, he had been hired by famed Banff outfitter Tom Wilson. By 1907, the brothers formed their own guiding company and in 1909 they relocated to the Athabasca River Valley, two years before the Brewsters. In particular, it was their reputation for backcountry survival skills that made the Ottos the first choice of many explorers and mountaineers visiting the area. They guided Mary Schäffer (1911), Dr. Charles Walcott (1913), and Sir Arthur Conan Doyle (1914), as well as American author James Oliver Curwood, whose subsequent novels paid homage to the wild Canadian landscape. Curwood's tales told of bears, wild mountain men, and plucky women who dared to trade the safety of civilized society for the unruly wilds of nature. Curwood even immortalized Bruce Otto in one of his books, *The Grizzly King*. During the early years of the Alpine Club of Canada, the Otto brothers were listed as official club outfitters.

Another of the earliest guiding and outfitting businesses based in Jasper Forest Park was operated by Donald Nelson "Curly"

Phillips, nicknamed for his curly locks. He was born on April 15, 1884, in Dorset, Ontario. Curly's father, Daniel Alvin Phillips, was responsible for giving Curly an early start in outdoor education. By the age of 12, Curly was already managing his own trapline. He was also a master craftsman of boats, a skill he had learned under his father's guidance. It was a combination of these skills and his confidence that made Curly one of the park's most sought-after guides.

Like the Otto brothers, Curly arrived in the Athabasca River Valley in 1909, at the beginning of a new age of exploration. The timing was perfect on his part—the first thing a visitor required was a competent guide and someone to outfit him or her for the wilderness. Curly gained a reputation for being reliable, remaining calm in all types of unpredictable situations, and protecting his clients from wild animals. He also mastered the use of an axe—a prized quality in a road-less park with few trails. His skill was exceptional when it came to building canoes, cabins, and temporary bridges across rivers.

Curly's introduction to the Canadian Rockies was a chance encounter with the Reverend George Kinney, an avid climber who, like many others, devoted entire summers to climbing any and every elevated landform that crossed his path. The meeting took place in early 1909, when both Kinney and Curly had stopped at John Moberly's homestead, along the Athabasca River, to replenish supplies. At the time, Kinney knew that there was a feverish race to be the first to summit the highest peak in the Canadian Rockies, Mount Robson. There was talk that Arthur Wheeler was planning to attempt the feat at an upcoming Alpine Club of Canada camp. So Kinney, intent on being the first, did not think twice about asking the young man at Moberly's, who just happened to be sporting an Ontario Guides' Association badge, to be his guide and outfitter.

If Kinney had been a bit hasty in selecting his guide, then Phillips was equally hasty with his acceptance. Despite the treachery of record spring snow melts, Phillips and Kinney reached the

Curly Phillips in the 1930s.

Smokey River via Moose Pass and then passed Berg Lake before establishing a base camp under the gaze of Robson's impressive northwest face. At this time, in the shadow of such a mighty rock, Curly, a young man who had never climbed a mountain, must have realized that he and Kinney had underestimated a

Alfred Ostheimer

Alfred Ostheimer

While the names of many early Jasper mountaineers are well known today, the names of others who achieved equally impressive climbing records are not. One such man is Alfred J. Ostheimer (1908–1983), an American who reached the summit of Mount Temple in Banff National Park at the tender age of 15. The following year, Ostheimer made successful first ascents of four mountains, including Mount Hooker with famed mountaineers J. Monroe Thorington and Hans Fuhrer.

In 1927, aged just 19, he returned to Jasper. That summer, employing Curly Phillips as an outfitter, Hans Fuhrer as a guide, and Adam Joachim as a horse packer, he travelled to the Columbia Icefield and climbed over 30 mountains in just 63 days; incredibly, he made 27 first ascents during this expedition. At the time, Ostheimer was a geology student at Harvard University and used the mountaineering expedition as a credit for his studies. But after completing schooling, he entered the insurance business and did not return to the Canadian Rockies until 1977, 50 years after completing what famed American alpinist Henry Hall described as "perhaps the greatest tour de force ever accomplished in a single season in the Canadian Rockies."

most formidable opponent. Over the next two weeks, Curly and Kinney made four attempts to reach the summit. They endured bad weather, a lack of ice climbing equipment, a shortage of food, and inadequate shelter. Their final attempt, on August 13, 1909, was literally a blind dash upwards as they attempted to get ahead of an approaching snowstorm. Amidst a whiteout, exhausted after 12 hours of difficult climbing and thin air, they reached what they thought to be the summit. Kinney quickly built a cairn to mark their success and then they began the even more difficult descent.

After returning to civilization, Kinney paid a visit to Wheeler to register his claim as the first to summit Mount Robson. Wheeler was immediately skeptical as Kinney had a reputation for embellishment. Kinney's claim was conspicuously omitted from the club's journal of first ascents that year. Kinney of course called Wheeler jealous, while Wheeler called Kinney's credibility into question. In 1911, in an attempt to make amends, Wheeler invited Kinney and Curly to attend the club's summer camp at Mount Robson, where hopefully another attempt would be made. According to one historian, it was during this camp that other climbers found Kinney's cairn below the true summit.

In regards to Kinney's summit attempt with Curly Phillips, renowned author and historian Chic Scott states that "they did not get to the top, but from where they were, they thought they were on the summit because of the mist and clouds. There was no malice, they just thought they were on the top." At the time, however, the controversy over Kinney's claim was big news in the climbing community. Curly, however, only benefited from the notoriety of the expedition.

Soon after his summit attempt of Mount Robson, Curly was endorsed by the Alpine Club of Canada as one of its official outfitters, which was also a huge boost for business. In the summer of 1911, Curly outfitted a joint Alpine Club of Canada–Smithsonian Institution expedition to the Mount Robson region that included such luminaries as Austrian mountaineer Conrad Kain; surveyor Arthur O. Wheeler; and a group of scientists

Curly Phillips at his home on Geikie Street.

working under direction from palaeontologist Dr. Charles
Walcott, who is credited with discovering the Burgess Shale in
Yoho National Park.

At the conclusion of the 1924 summer guiding season, Curly
married Grace Inkster, whom he had met at a skating party in
Edmonton. Inkster was a member of a pioneering family who had
homesteaded the King Edward Park area, southeast of downtown,
as early as the 1870s. The couple had three children: Sam (born
in 1928), Joy (1930), and Ivy (1932). They lived in a home at 315
Geikie Street that Curly built for his family.

Having completed a very expensive rail line, the GTP embarked
on an aggressive publicity campaign and encouraged tourists to
visit Jasper Forest Park—and to arrive by train, of course. The
railway company and Jasper Park Collieries felt there was potential
for the Pocahontas area, east of the divisional point, as a tourist
destination. The nearby hot springs were a major attraction,
Punchbowl Falls created a scenic diversion from the coal mining
settlement, and people could have picnics along the many streams.
In 1911, the GTP had Francis Rattenbury, the architect of
Victoria's Empress Hotel, design a sprawling château-like hotel
at the confluence of the Athabasca and Fiddle rivers. Rattenbury's

Alpine Club of Canada

Although most Canadians were unfamiliar with the sport of mountain climbing at the beginning of the last century, it did not take long for adventurous locals to aspire to great heights. The impetus for a burgeoning popularity in the sport was set in motion when Arthur Oliver Wheeler, an avid mountaineer and also a renowned surveyor, joined forces with Elizabeth Parker, a journalist with the *Manitoba Free Press* who had a love for mountains, to form the Alpine Club of Canada (ACC) in 1906. A list of early club members reads like a who's who of the Canadian Rockies—Morrison Bridgland, Conrad Kain, Bill Peyto, Tom Wilson, Byron Harmon, Mary Schäffer—names familiar to anyone who spends time in the region.

Much of the club's early attention was focused around Banff National Park and British Columbia's Selkirk Mountains. But after Jasper Forest Park was established in 1907, a whole new world of mountains was opened.

Curly Phillips (2nd from left) was a popular ACC guide.

Today, like similar clubs in the United States and Great Britain, the ACC is a nonprofit mountaineering organization whose objectives include encouraging mountaineering through educational programs, exploring and studying alpine and glacial regions, and preserving mountain flora and fauna. The club's ongoing projects include operating the Canadian Alpine Centre (Lake Louise Hostel), maintaining a system of huts throughout the backcountry of the Canadian Rockies, and publishing the annual *Canadian Alpine Journal*.

The first bathhouse at Miette Hot Springs was completed in 1913.

Sir Arthur Conan Doyle (back; 2nd from left) on a picnic with his family and guides beside the Athabasca River.

sketches, along with plans for a townsite and a proposed carriage road up to the hot springs, were approved by the government. Although the hotel was never built due to financial difficulties faced by the GTP, a Dominion Land Survey party laid out the route for a carriage road leading up to the hot springs from the Athabasca River Valley that passed by Punchbowl Falls. The road was completed in 1913, and a small log bathhouse was constructed at what had become known as Miette Hot Springs.

The highlight of the GTP publicity campaign was the summer of 1914, when the GTP invited Sir Arthur Conan Doyle, world-famous author of the beloved detective series *Sherlock Holmes*, to take a tour on Canada's newest transcontinental rail line. The railway company ensured that Doyle's journey was well documented by the media—in Canada, the United States, and even Europe.

Unlike the CPR, the GTP did not build grandiose hotels upon completion of its track, which left Jasper without suitable accommodations for a traveller of Doyle's social stature. So the GTP offered Doyle its executive train for travel and accommodation. The train provided luxurious sleeping quarters, a dining car, and a lounging car. It was also equipped with an experienced crew that included porters and a chef.

After departing Edmonton on June 11, 1914, Doyle and his wife, Lady Jean Doyle, and their three children, were greeted at the Jasper Railway Station by Colonel Samuel Maynard Rogers, Jasper's first resident superintendent, whom Doyle had previously met in Africa during the Boer Wars. The two old friends set out on horseback along the trails around Jasper along with park warden Alex McDougall and Edmonton photographer William James Topley, who ensured every aspect of Doyle's journey was recorded.

On one of their adventures, they travelled by horseback along the Athabasca River guided by Closson Otto and Jimmie Rootes. While stopping for lunch, Doyle was inspired to compose a poem titled *The Athabasca Trail*. In his poem, Doyle extolled the virtue of the noble horse packer. Although no one knows exactly which one of the guides Doyle immortalized, perhaps the diplomatic poet honoured both men by leaving the packer unnamed.

Doyle and his party also visited Pyramid Lake while travelling along a newly constructed trail that could easily accommodate a horse-drawn carriage. Doyle had been asked by the government to lay out a nine-hole golf course between the town and the lake that had been surveyed and divided into lots. Two months after Doyle's visit, however, World War I was declared and all plans for development in the park were put on hold, including Doyle's golf course.

Doyle Returns

Sherlock Holmes creator Arthur Conan Doyle first visited Jasper in 1914, and although his original trip was more business than pleasure, he was affected by the park's beauty and returned for a second visit in 1923. Doyle and his family stayed at the Jasper Park Lodge, and he left this well-read anecdote in the guest book:

"A New York man reached Heaven and as he passed the gate, Peter said, 'I am sure you will like it.' A Pittsburgh man followed, and Peter said, 'It will be a very great change for you.' Finally there came a man from Jasper Park. 'I am afraid,' said Peter, 'that you will be disappointed.'"

6 Growth

At the same time the railway began bringing the first tourists to Jasper Forest Park, plans were drawn up to establish a town. For decades previously, towns across Canada were built beside newly laid railway track and were often laid out in a symmetrical grid pattern. Edouard Deville, the Surveyor General of Canada, described an initial government plan for Fitzhugh, as the settlement was still called, as "a common grid-iron pattern of the real estate man, made to focus on 95 acres of rail yards. It is devoid of any characteristic or attractive feature and ignores every principal of town planning." Deville felt that as a potential tourist destination the town, needed to be different, subsequently submitting his own plan, using the natural features of the landscape to denote the town limits.

In 1913, the settlement comprised of nothing more than a row of tents and ramshackle wood buildings scattered along the railway track. One of these wooden structures was the Hotel Fitzhugh, owned by a Mr. Stevenson, which burned to the ground in December 1913. The few government employees living in the park were staying in log cabins originally built for railway engineers. As they were not designed to be permanent, nor were they suitable for Colonel Rogers and his family, an official park administration building was planned, one that would serve as a home for the park superintendent and as headquarters of park operations. Located across from the railway station, it was also envisioned to be a welcoming sight for visitors as they disembarked from their trains. In order to accomplish this, the government hired respected Edmonton architect Alfred M. Calderon. Calderon's final design, a rustic yet elegant log cabin, was the perfect marriage between function and nature.

Digging the foundation for the new administration building was more difficult than first anticipated. The ground was filled with rocks of all shapes, sizes, and colours that had been rounded by glacial and water action. Once they had been painstakingly excavated, the rocks were piled up around the construction site. Seeing the piles of rounded rocks, Colonel Rogers suggested

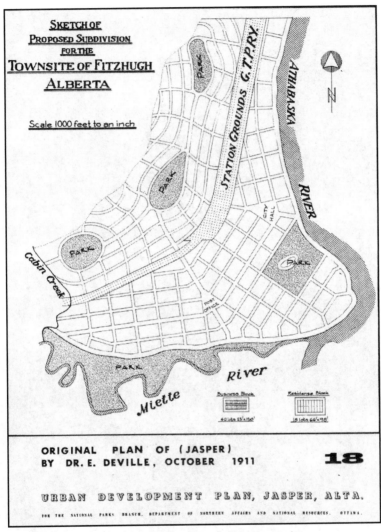

Deville's 1911 town plan held elements that remain in place today.

that they be used as part of the building's construction. His idea struck a chord with Dominion Parks Branch commissioner, James Harkin, and Calderon, the designing architect, which led to a construction that was a combination of log and stone. When the building was completed in 1913, Colonel Rogers, along with his

The townsite of Jasper, soon after the park administration building was completed in 1914.

The Robson's home at its original location on Geikie Street.

409 Patricia Street

The town of Jasper is blessed with many historic homes, but the trim, two-storey building at 409 Patricia Street is the only one that was moved, in an effort to protect the historic resource from demolition. Originally located at 808 Geikie Street, the 1919 building was designed by Edmonton architect Alfred M. Calderon, who also designed the park administration building, the building currently occupied by Jasper Camera & Gift, and Jasper's Anglican church.

John Salisbury (Jack) Robson was born in England in 1871 and immigrated to Canada in the 1890s. After reaching the Klondike in search of gold, he married Mary Bowers and established an outfitting business in Banff. In 1910, he made his way north to the Athabasca River Valley where he worked as a park warden from 1914 to 1919; he then worked for the CNR until his retirement. In 1919, the Robsons and their five children moved into their new two-storey home on Geikie Street. One of Jack and Mary's daughters, Joan, was fascinated by the beauty and delicacy of the park's wildflowers and began recording their beauty in watercolour. Her artwork became so well known that she was granted a special license from the government to pick wildflowers within the park.

Today, the Robson's home is the administration office for the Jasper Chamber of Commerce, and Joan's wildflower collections and paintings are held by the Jasper Yellowhead Museum and Archives.

wife Annie and their adopted daughter moved into the ground floor. Offices were located on the east wing and on the second level. The original plan also showed a museum on the second level, but this was never incorporated into the finished building.

At the time that the park administration building opened in 1914, there was little townsite development beyond a wagon road that ran parallel to the railway track (now Connaught Drive) and Jasper's total population was around 125. Hugh Matheson, who had been employed by the Department of the Interior to create a topographical survey of Jasper Forest Park in 1911, was asked to expand on the original Deville townsite plan. Matheson's first draft, however, consisted of a grid pattern. After much discussion and compromise, a town plan that combined elements from

Carved in the Haida Gwaii in the 1880s, the Raven totem pole arrived in Jasper by train and was erected in front of the railway station around 1915. Due to safety issues, the pole was removed in 2009; it was replaced in 2011 by the Two Brothers totem pole.

Deville's original, fluid design and Matheson's more traditional grid was approved by Deville, the surveyor general, on June 5, 1914. Colonel Rogers, a proud military man, named the main street after the Duke of Connaught, a son of Queen Victoria who had a long and well-regarded military career and took office as Governor General of Canada in 1911. The street running parallel to the main street was named for the Duke's daughter, Princess Patricia. Rogers also named many other streets, many for natural features such as mountains and rivers, as well as for trees native to the park.

Over the next few years, a number of buildings were constructed along Connaught Drive. When passengers alighted at the railway station, they were greeted by picturesque storefronts and local merchants eagerly awaiting their arrival. Some of the first businesses to open along Connaught Drive were Stewart's Store, a pool hall, Mah Hay's Restaurant, Dr. Niven's Drugstore (which opened in 1912 and was Jasper's first official postal outlet), and the W.S. Jeffery Store. The latter, at 410 Connaught Drive, is the only commercial building along the main road that survives from this era (it is now Sayuri Japanese Restaurant).

Willard S. Jeffery was typical of Jasper's first businessmen. Originally from Nova Scotia, Jeffery headed west and established temporary general stores to serve railway construction crews. He arrived in the Athabasca River Valley around 1911, and reached the construction camp at Mile 112 in 1911, ahead of the actual railway. Jeffery's first store served the needs of railway workers and by 1929 had grown into W.S. Jeffery and Sons Grocery and Gents Furnishings. It was an imposing building for the day with a wide variety of goods available for sale, including food, hardware, sporting, clothing, and outfitting supplies.

One block back from Connaught Drive, Jasper Rooms, the precursor to today's Athabasca Hotel, opened in 1915. More of a boarding house than a hotel, it was two separate buildings owned by the Woolley family, who rented rooms on the second floors and operated a grocery store and rented space to the Imperial

The original Athabasca Hotel opened in 1921.

Bank of Canada at street level. In 1921, the two buildings were joined together, painted, and renamed the Athabasca Hotel. The red brick hotel that stands on the site today, best known as the Atha-B, was built by the Calgary Brewing and Malt Company in 1928. The earliest guests paid between $1.50 and $2.50 for a room with a shared bathroom, and were able to relax in the elegant lobby, which was decorated with leather seating, trophy heads, and exotic palms.

As tourist numbers increased, the park did not have adequate accommodations, especially for wealthy tourists. In an effort to rectify this, Robert C. Lett of the GTP began urging Robert Kenneth of the Edmonton Tent and Mattress Company to build a tent camp in the vicinity of the railway station. Fred and Jack Brewster, who knew the area well through their guiding business, recommended an ideal site along the shore of Lac Beauvert, across the Athabasca River from the townsite. What was originally known as Tent City opened for the summer of 1915. Each of the 10 sturdy canvas tents had a wooden floor, and a dining room was contained within a much larger tent.

Tent City proved to be a success during its first summer and was mentioned in the government's 1915–1916 annual report: "The Grand Trunk Pacific Company advertised the park considerably this last summer and as at present there is no hotel at Jasper, a summer camp called The Tented City was opened on the borders of lake Beau Vert, under the management of Mr. Kenneth of the Edmonton Tent and Mattress Company. It proved a success, and over two hundred and sixty visitors registered at this camp alone, and availed themselves of this accommodation to explore Jasper park and vicinity. It is proposed to organize a similar camp on a larger scale this summer." The 1916–1917 government report also noted that Tent City was well patronized considering the war conditions that prevailed.

While Colonel Rogers was very specific about the appearance of new buildings along Connaught Drive, in the case of the pool hall, it was a notorious reputation that concerned the superintendent. The hall was a gathering place for crib tournaments, which seemed harmless enough, but they often attracted some of Jasper's seedier characters. Late at night during one tournament in January, 1915, word reached the pool hall that the police barracks on Geikie

Tent City opened on the shore of Lac Beauvert in 1915.

Street was on fire. Everyone rushed up to watch the blaze, and old Jim Campbell, who had spent many a night locked up, is reputed to have been standing next to the lone policeman in town when he said, "You'll never get me in that place again." Meanwhile, the original pool hall was replaced by the more aesthetically pleasing, two-storey Otto's Hall in 1917 (a new façade was added in 1935 and the property is now Bearfoot in the Park).

Recognizing a need for a more respectable form of entertainment than gambling or drinking, Colonel Rogers wholeheartedly approved Jack Donnelly's application for a movie theatre. Colonel Rogers was not the only local who was eager to see an alternate form of entertainment; in 1922 the newly formed CNR donated cash to be put towards construction costs and generously pledged to provide a permanent source of electricity for the theatre. Officially opened in 1923, Jasper's first movie theatre screened silent films and had a stage for the fledgling Jasper Theatrical Society to perform live theatre. There was also a piano, played by local women, which brought depth and dimension to the silent movies of the day.

Colonel Rogers was also concerned about the haphazard way in which stables and corrals operated by outfitters and guides were scattered through the town. He felt that their consistently untidy appearance and often unpleasant smell would not be appreciated by tourists. Rogers understood the importance of the barns to tourism but did not think that they needed to be right in the middle of town; therefore, he set aside a dedicated area along the northern edge of the town on what is now Bonhomme Street for the outfitters, the warden stables, and a blacksmith shop. Some of the early outfitters to make use of the corral lots were Alex Wylie, the Otto brothers, Curly Phillips, and the Brewster brothers.

In addition to the administration building, Calderon was responsible for designing a number of private residences, including for Fred Brewster, whose home on the corner of Pyramid Lake Road and Bonhomme Street was completed in 1925. The following year, RCMP barracks were constructed at the corner of

Robson Street and Elm Avenue, with a nearby building designed for married officers. Government records before this time show that officers were officially stationed at Pocahontas and Jasper as early as 1913, but little is known beyond their names: Calow, Bryant, Thornwall, McGillicuddy, MacDonald.

The Stanley Wright Industrial Park, across the rail line from downtown, also dates to the 1920s. Its genesis was the Edmonton-

Jasper's original fire station

Jasper Fire Station

In 1914, Dougald MacLachlan, a local contractor, built Jasper's first fire station. Costing $1,000, it was a one-storey log building on the corner of Geikie Street and Elm Avenue (where the elementary school is today). It housed the government's fire extinguishing apparatus and had living quarters for a caretaker. Whenever there was a fire, it would be attended by government employees and local volunteers, who were all issued with leather hats and rubber boots (they did not receive any compensation for clothes that were lost while battling a fire).

At the time, the government was primarily concerned with the suppression of forest fires, as illustrated in this 1914 letter from the park superintendent to the Dominion Parks Branch: "The fire conditions could not be worse than they are at present, as we have an extremely dry spell and there is a very heavy fire based Hayward Lumber Company, which established a lumber yard on the site in the mid-1920s. The area was officially surveyed in 1950, when seven lots were established. A revised 1952 survey increased the lot numbers, while also including a planned power plant and space for a concrete mixing plant and auto repair shops. Today, there are 52 lots zoned for industrial use and the precinct is named for Jasper's townsite manager between 1970 and 1988.

raging in B.C. to the west and south, which would seem to be on Thompson valley . . . I have had our own Volunteer Fire Brigade practicing with the fire apparatus, in case of a local emergency, and if necessary will turn every man on to fire work, shutting down all works but those of necessary trail extension, to enable me to reach threatened areas."

In 1936, the original fire hall was replaced with a larger building on the corner of Elm Avenue and Patricia Street, behind the Park Administration Building. At the same time, the Jasper Volunteer Fire Brigade (JVFB) was formed. Today, the JVFB has 30 members and is overseen by a fire chief and a deputy fire chief.

In the mid-1990s, a government report suggested that the configuration of the 1936 fire hall was not suited to the larger size of modern emergency vehicles, and that more space was needed. Construction on the new Jasper Emergency Services Building (JESB) at 518 Geikie Street began on October 15, 2000. Completed in July, 2002, the new building was around four times as large as the original fire hall and provided space for ambulance and fire services, and an area that can be set aside as a command centre for large-scale disasters. The original 1936 fire hall now holds the Brushfire Art Gallery and a yoga studio.

1936 fire hall

The Jasper Emergency Services Building was completed in 2002.

The lodging at Lac Beauvert that had opened in 1915 as Tent City was becoming more popular each year, and there were many days when the train arrived with eager tourists who had to be turned away. The Brewster brothers, who had purchased the property after World War I, were not interested in expanding the camp any further or becoming hoteliers, so in 1921, they sold Tent City to the CNR, which was anxious to establish a flagship resort at Jasper that could compete with CPR resorts like the Banff Springs. The railway company began adding log cabins, and in June 1922, Jasper Park Lodge officially opened. The following year, additional cabins and a main lodge, which the CNR advertised as the "world's largest single storey log structure," were added. The main lodge housed a ballroom, a formal lobby with a dining room, and lounges where guests could enjoy sweeping mountain views. Along the lakeshore was an outdoor dance pavilion that reached out over the emerald waters of Lac Beauvert. The guest cabins featured porches decorated with pieces of gnarled wood formed into decorative designs. The main lodge and the guest cabins were decorated with rustic furniture, trophy heads, and handcrafted woodwork. It did not take long for the charms of Jasper Park Lodge to gain an international reputation as one of the world's most luxurious wilderness resorts.

As president of the CNR, Sir Henry Thornton visited the new Jasper Park Lodge in 1923. Being an ardent golfer, he decided the growing resort town needed a first-class golf course to give it the distinction he desired. Thornton turned to a young Canadian golf course architect who was rapidly making an impressive reputation for himself. The architect was Stanley Thompson, and with his commissioning in Jasper, the die was cast for the future of golf course design in Canada.

When he accepted Thornton's request to look over the possibilities in Jasper in May 1924, Thompson was at once taken with the exceptional views that the landscape offered. However, he was astute enough to realize that views alone did not make for an excellent course. In an article written for *Canadian Golfer*

Cavell Tea Room

Fred H. Slark came to Jasper in 1921 as an official photographer for the CNR. He and his wife, Gladys, opened a small curio shop in the main lounge area of the Jasper Park Lodge where they sold his photographs as postcards, along with souvenirs and boxed chocolates.

In 1922, the Slarks gained permission to build a tea room at the base of Mount Edith Cavell. At this time, Cavell Road, had not been completed, so a temporary tea room opened around 26 kilometres from the valley floor.

In 1927, Cavell Road was completed and the Slarks moved their operation to the end of the road, directly below Mount Edith Cavell. Although narrow, steep, and winding, the new road was very popular with visitors, which made it an ideal spot for a light meal. Slark roughed out a frame for the planned log cabin before tragedy struck. With Fred Rutis, a close friend and experienced Swiss alpine guide, in August 1927, he headed into the Tonquin Valley to attempt the

Cavell Tea Room

first ascent of Redoubt Peak, one of the Ramparts. After successfully reaching the summit, the two friends fell to their deaths on the descent and their bodies were never found.

In honour of her husband's memory, Gladys carried on with the plans for the tea room and completed it by the end of the following summer. It became popular not only with tourists but also with locals, who would negotiate the tortuous Cavell Road just to enjoy a cup of tea and a slice of Mrs. Slark's orange bread. In 1946, the tea room was sold to Don and Anne Guild, who added guest rooms and renamed it Mt. Cavell Chalet. Tea and orange bread remained a Jasper tradition until the building was demolished in 1976.

on his design at Jasper spoke of his philosophy on this matter: "The principle observed in planning the course has been that the golf should be sufficiently high-class to justify itself apart altogether from the extraordinary setting in which the course is being placed." Thompson's solution was to design a course that American

Stanley Thompson

It has been said that no golfer has made more of an impression on Canada than Stanley Thompson, a larger-than-life character known as the "Toronto Terror" (some say for his golfing prowess, others for his business acumen). According to *Golf In Canada, A History*, by Canadian golf historian James A. Barclay, "Between 1920 and 1953, this Canadian amateur golfer turned golf architect sculpted out of farmland, heath, forest, and mountain some of the finest and most scenic golf courses in the world." He is credited with the design of at least 125 courses, 100 of them in Canada, but nowhere did he achieve such success and fame as he did first in the Canadian Rockies.

Thompson was born in Toronto in 1893, one of five golfing brothers. He and his brothers won many national titles between them in the 1920s. At an early age, he began caddying under the noted professional George Cumming at the Toronto Golf Club. Thompson's education apparently included a turf management course at the Ontario Agricultural College in Guelph, showing he had an interest in Cumming's other activity—golf course architecture, but he was drawn away by World War I to serve with the Royal Canadian Artillery, where he became a commissioned officer and was mentioned in dispatches for gallantry.

Upon returning from overseas in 1919, he pursued his career as an amateur golfer but also joined forces with his brother Nicol, professional at the Hamilton Golf Club, and Cumming, to form the golf course design firm of Thompson, Cumming and Thompson. Due to the pent-up demand for new golf courses created by the war, the early 1920s were a time of huge opportunity for accomplished architects, and the new company flourished. By early 1922, Thompson could afford to go out on his own, and he created Stanley Thompson & Co., "Golf and Landscape Engineers, Architects." In addition to the Jasper Park Lodge Golf Course, he designed famous layouts such as the Banff Springs Golf Course (1928; Banff, Alberta), St. George's Golf and Country Club (1928; Toronto, Ontario), Capilano Golf Club (1937; Vancouver, British Columbia), and Highlands Links (1938; Cape Breton Island, Nova Scotia). His designs were significant for their use of natural features, a throwback to links courses of Scotland. Irregular bunkers on direct lines between tee and green and holes aligned with distant mountains are also classic Thompson traits.

By the time Thompson designed Highlands Links in 1938, he had become known as much for his golf course design as for his flamboyant attire, his love of whiskey, and his colourful stories. Thompson died in 1953, penniless after losing multiple fortunes. To those he owed money, his debts were forgiven for the joy he had given them all over the years, or so the story goes.

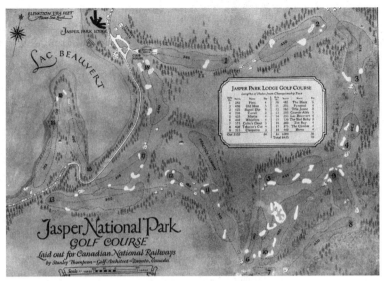

Thompson's original layout of Jasper Park Lodge Golf Course.

golf architect Robert Trent Jones, later a partner with Thompson, described as being of the "heroic school." Trent Jones postulated that until this time, golf courses had been built following one of two basic designs—the "strategic," like many of the original Scottish links courses, and the "penal," like the famous Oakmont course in the United States where bunkers were numerous and there was a call for accuracy rather than distance. The heroic was a combination of the strategic and the penal and forced the golfer to make a decision about how much penalty was associated with a diagonal hazard and how much of it he or she could avoid with shot-making abilities. Thompson's course at Jasper was only one of a handful in North America that Trent Jones considered met this ideal.

The site was covered in a dense forest and littered with massive boulders, but after spending many months surveying the property, Thompson brought in 200 men and 50 teams of horses to clear the land and begin shaping the wilderness into a premier golf course. The first nine holes were ready for play in 1925, and the full 18-hole course opened in 1926. Designing the Jasper Park

Lodge Golf Course propelled Thompson into the upper echelon of golf course architects (he later designed the Banff Springs Golf Course), and his work has proved timeless; celebrities such as Bing Crosby have made regular golf trips to Jasper and the course is consistently ranked as one of the world's best.

Although Jasper was a bustling town by 1925, it was still in the heart of a remote wilderness, with the vast majority of visitors arriving by train from Edmonton. The region south of Jasper, including the Columbia Icefield, was rarely visited, with only a rough horse trail linking Jasper to Banff. Overlooking the Columbia Icefield, Mount Alberta, the highest peak in its namesake province, remained unclimbed until Yuko Maki, an ambitious Japanese mountaineer decided to travel to Canada and climb the great peak. Fellow members of the Japanese Alpine Club participating in the expedition included S. Hashimoto (geologist), Yukio Mita (botanist and sketch artist), N. Okabe (photographer), and T. Hayakawa (medic). After arriving in Vancouver, they travelled by train to Jasper, where they prepared for the climb while staying at the Jasper Park Lodge. They hired Fred Brewster as an outfitter and two professional Swiss guides, Heinrich Fuhrer and Hans Kohler. Extra hands on the expedition included Jean Weber, another skilled Swiss guide, and Jasper local George Camp. Six days after leaving Jasper Park Lodge, they reached the head of Habel Creek, where a base camp was established. From this point, it took three days to reach a point within striking distance of the summit. Before dawn the following morning, the group departed for a full day of technical climbing and eventually reached the summit late in the afternoon. As darkness was approaching, they quickly built a cairn to enclose an ice axe given to Maki by the Emperor of Japan as well as papers signed to mark their accomplishment and then safely descended.

By the mid-1920s, the golden era of guiding was coming to an end in the Canadian Rockies, so Curly Phillips found employment as Brewster's Maligne Lake camp manager. In addition to his duties around the chalet, Curly spent his time building a boat.

Legend of the Silver Ice Axe

When Yuko Maki and his team reached the summit of Mount Alberta in 1925, Maki built a rock cairn, below which he left papers signed to mark their accomplishment and an ice axe that had been given to him by the Emperor of Japan. Although stories of a solid silver axe left at the top of Mount Alberta began to spread, it was not found until 1948, when two American climbers, Fred Ayers and John Oberlin, reached the summit—they were the second group to do so. They recovered the spike of the legendary axe, but as Oberlin wrote in the 1949 edition of the *American Alpine Journal*, "The axe was not silver but a good Swiss make, weather-beaten and rusty . . . Since the spike and ferrule were frozen in solid black ice between the lower rocks of the cairn . . . We were determined to take it with us, partly because we felt that it should be preserved in the museum of one of the Alpine Clubs, but particularly because Fred needed an axe for the return along the ridge to the notch . . . "

In 1965, students from Nagano Boys High School arrived in Jasper National Park to climb Mount Alberta as a way of commemorating the 40th anniversary of Maki's ascent. At the top, they found the handle of the axe that Ayers and Oberlin had been unable to get out of the ice and brought it back down the mountain.

In the early 1990s, Jasper resident Greg Horne, a long-time Parks Canada employee and a member of the ACC, was visiting the American Alpine Club archives in New York to research the original 1925 ascent of Mount Alberta, when he found the spike recovered by Oberlin and Ayers in a box labelled "Mount Alberta 1948." In 2000, when a group of Japanese and Canadian climbers made a commemorative 75th anniversary climb of Mount Alberta, the two halves of the axe were united and placed on permanent display at the Jasper Yellowhead Museum and Archives.

He had built his first boat for Brewster in 1920, but this one was larger and would be the first with a motor to be used on Maligne Lake. Six metres long and seating 24 passengers, it could easily reach Samson Narrows (Spirit Island) in a few hours, something that had not been possible in the past.

The scenic cruises proved so popular that Curly applied for his own tour boat concession. After being granted permission, he set

The iconic boathouse at Maligne Lake was completed in 1929.

Fish Stocking

Although the government first began looking into stocking lakes in the Canadian Rockies specifically for the purpose of sport fishing soon after the creation of Banff National Park, in 1885, it was not for another 30 years that stocking was considered in Jasper, where glacier-fed lakes did not support natural populations of fish. The earliest study of Jasper's fishless lakes was undertaken in 1925 by a group of scientists from the University of Manitoba, with the assistance of the Department of Marine and Fisheries and the Biological Board of Canada.

With positive reports, stocking began in the late 1920s with the release of brown trout fry in small lakes close to the Jasper townsite, including Lakes Edith, Annette, and Mildred. To allow the fry time to grow, these lakes were then closed to fishing for two years. Maligne Lake was first stocked in 1928, when 190,000 brook trout fry were transported by packhorse up the Maligne Valley. Similar numbers were released over ensuing years, and by 1932, trout measuring up to 46 centimetres (18 inches) were being reported in Maligne Lake.

The park's first hatchery was an old cabin beside Cabin Creek, but the operation had been relocated to the basement of the Park Administration Building (now the Park Visitor Centre) by 1930.

As the park's stocking program became too large for the basement of the Administration Building, a purpose-built hatchery was opened in 1942 on the Maligne River, just upstream from its confluence with the Athabasca River. Fingerlings hatched at this facility were released into Medicine and Maligne Lakes, as well as lakes throughout western Canada's national parks. By this time, fishing was a major draw in Jasper National Park, and Maligne Lake was the focus of anglers from around the world. The decision to close the hatchery in 1973 was met with resistance from many locals, including the Jasper Chamber of Commerce and the local fish and game association, but the end of the stocking program did not mark the end of fishing in the park, which is still a popular pastime for both locals and visitors.

A fish hatchery operated beside the
Maligne River between 1942 and 1973.

to work building a boathouse along the same stretch of lakeshore as the Brewster dock. It was supported by log pilings driven into the shallow water at the lakeshore with planked decking. The actual building was of post-and-beam construction; it was 12 metres (40 feet) wide and 15 metres (50 feet) long and topped by a shingle roof. Completed in 1929, the structure was entirely in keeping with the government's architectural guidelines and remains an iconic building to this day.

Soon after opening the boathouse, Curly built the cedar-planked *Leah*, which was named for the wife of Samson Beaver, who had drawn the map that helped Schäffer find the lake two decades previously. The boat remained in service until the 1970s. Twelve passengers could be seated on the wooden bench that ran down the centre of the boat; blankets were offered on cooler days.

At the same time Curly was building his boathouse, the government began stocking Maligne Lake with trout. This attracted anglers—a new breed of visitors who were anxious to rent boats. They rented boats from Curly for $0.50 for the first hour and $0.25 for each hour after or at a flat rate of $2.00 per day. By this time, Curly had erected simple tent cabins near his boathouse, which offered accommodation and food for up to 25 guests at one time at what he advertised as Rainbow Camp. His brother (Harry), his father (Alvin), his brother-in-law (Bert Wilkins), as well as Jasper locals such as Adam Joachim, who was a descendant of one of the region's first fur traders, helped him run his camp. The earliest promotional brochures for Curly's Rainbow Camp boasted of fishing, boating, summer skiing, and mountain climbing.

While Curly was establishing a presence at Maligne Lake, Fred Brewster was expanding his own tourist operation at the lake, with Shovel Pass Lodge opening in the early 1920s as of part of Brewster's Rocky Mountain Camps and his Maligne Lake Chalet opening in 1927. Fitting perfectly with the government's aesthetic vision for architecture within the park, the chalet was a single-storey building of horizontal logs with a gabled roof. Overnight guests were accommodated in adjacent tent cabins, and the chalet contained a dining room, kitchen, and communal living space.

Meanwhile, in 1924, Jasper's original GTP station burned to the ground. The CNR immediately began planning for a new station, one that would cost $300,000 in the end—an enormous amount of money at the time. The design was a tribute to the popular Arts and Crafts movement—a custard-coloured stucco exterior, multi-paned windows, and cedar shingles gave the station a cottage-like appearance. In keeping with the architectural example set by various government buildings around the town of Jasper, the lower portion of the station featured local river stone. The interior was typical of the day—the large common area was sparse and rustic although a large fireplace kept passengers warm and comfortable.

The Harragin Sisters

While names such as Brewster, Otto, and Phillips are well known in Jasper, few people have heard of Agnes and Mona Harragin, the first female guides to be licensed in a Canadian national park. Agnes and Mona were born in 1904 and 1906 respectively, in Port au Spain, Trinidad, and moved to British Columbia as young children. Barely out of their teens, the two plucky girls found employment managing Fred Brewster's camp at Medicine Lake in 1927. The following summer, they were keen to begin guiding, as this diary entry shows:

. . . Of course the beginning of 1928 stands out in my memory because I was starting on a new job in a new location. In the early spring of that year, I received a letter from Brewster's office offering the job of cook and hostess to Mona and me, also giving us the privilege of choosing any Brewster camp in the park . . . Both of us did a great deal of thinking with Mona finally suggesting that we just simply write back saying that, unless we could guide, we would not be returning to Jasper for the tourist season. Secretly we decided that, if we were refused, we would write back immediately accepting the previous offer, picking Maligne Lake camp. I will never forget my inward feelings when a reply came back stating that both of us would be hired on as guides for the "Circle Trip," with our base camp at Medicine Lake . . . Incidentally, later in that year, I learned that Mrs. Brewster had insisted that girls should be given a trial run on guiding because, she for one, would far rather make the round trip with one of her own kind as guide. She suggested that a number of other women would be of the same opinion.

The station also contained a restaurant called The Beanery, and the women who worked there became known as "Beanery Queens." The second floor was used for staff accommodations.

In addition to overseeing the development of the Jasper townsite, Colonel Rogers had an important role to play in wildlife management. Although now understood to be very complex, many of the human-wildlife strategies Colonel Rogers applied were based on observations provided by park wardens; he had little concern for the natural balance of the park's ecosystems. During this era, the aim was to provide the visiting public with the best viewing experience (rather than providing the wildlife with the most natural environment possible); an early park directive instructed superintendents to "endeavor to exterminate all those

In 1928, they were indeed issued licences to guide guests from Jasper to Maligne Lake via Shovel Pass. In 1930, Agnes married Mark Truxler, another Brewster guide, and that same year Mona married Charlie Matheson, a park warden. Agnes and Mark lived for many years in the railway station at Old Entrance, just outside the eastern park boundary. For a time, they managed Miette Hot Springs and were then employed as caretakers at the East Park Gate. Mona and Charlie operated a trail riding operation in Jasper until 1940, when they established Circle M Guest Ranch, just outside the park's east gate.

Agnes (top right) and Mona (bottom left) were two of the park's original female guides.

Construction of the new Jasper Railway Station, 1925.

animals which prey upon others." Tourists were encouraged to interact with wild animals by giving them human foods and watching them feed at local dumps. Jasper even had a few animals that were essentially town pets. In the ensuing decades, bear sightings along park roads were often like carnival sideshows; tourists would try to entice the bruins into posing for pictures by offering them food.

One area of concern for Colonel Rogers was the rapidly decreasing number of elk in the park. For the most part, he did not seem too concerned about why the elk numbers were falling; the main question on his mind was how to increase their numbers. The blame for the loss of elk was conveniently placed on predators such as bears, coyotes, wolves, and cougars. These animals were seen as natural enemies of the park, and future wildlife management strategies focused on eliminating the threat of predators for the continued survival of large mammals like elk.

Colonel Rogers's solution to the elk problem was simple— he simply ordered more. Around 1920, he received approval to relocate an elk herd from Yellowstone National Park to Jasper. To Colonel Rogers, an elk was an elk—what difference did it make if it was from Yellowstone or Jasper? He assumed the new elk would simply replace the indigenous elk; however, the introduced elk ate different vegetation and made new trails, all the while multiplying profusely. Eventually, the park became so overpopulated with elk that there was not enough food to sustain their numbers, and a culling program was instituted.

Fire management was another important facet of early park doctrines. For centuries before the establishment of Jasper Forest Park, the Athabasca River Valley had been a natural fire corridor. Fire would sweep through the valley every so many years and burn

Bear Tales

Although grizzly and black bears are widespread through the Canadian Rockies, attacks on humans are rare. The very few cases of fatal attacks that have occurred in Jasper National Park include Percy Hamilton Goodair, a warden who was killed on patrol in Tonquin Valley, aged 52. Goodair was said to have been a well-educated Englishman who had previously served as a lieutenant in the Imperial Army during the South African Boer Wars. Like many war veterans, he found employment in Jasper under chief park warden Dick Langford. Goodair was considered punctual, so when he failed to return from a patrol in the Tonquin Valley in September 1929, Langford was immediately concerned. Three wardens were sent out to search for Goodair; they first checked his cabin and then spread out along surrounding trails. Unfortunately, by the time they found Goodair it was too late; he had been killed by a grizzly bear. They brought his remains back to the cabin and used wood from the front step to make a coffin. Goodair had been a member of the local Mason

A sign marks the burial site of bear attack victim Percy Goodair.

lodge, and in an unprecedented procession, his fellow Masons trekked out to Goodair's final resting place to honour him with a formal Mason's funeral and marked his grave with a poem. Goodair Peak, in adjoining Mount Robson Provincial Park, is named in his honour.

Connaught Drive, 1926. The second building from the left is now Jasper Camera & Gift.

Slim Henry riding Skyhigh to first place in the 1937 Jasper Rodeo.

Jasper Heritage Rodeo

A rodeo may not seem like an event that would be held in the wilderness of the Canadian Rockies, but the Jasper Heritage Rodeo perfectly reflects the cowboy culture of Jasper's past.

The first rodeo in Jasper was hosted by the Jasper Horseman's Association in 1926. It was held at Henry House Flats, northeast of town, and the records show that Jack Cooper rode Dynamite and won first place in the bucking horse contest. Dan Bowles was second on Bang Tail and Abe Reimer third on Rolling Pin. Alex Wylie won the cowboy barrel race, Dan Giles took second, and Charles Bowlen third. Dean Swift, one of Lewis Swift's children, teamed up with Don Giles to win the inaugural packing competition. Each winner received a replica of a trophy, designed by Azalea Brewster, Fred Brewster's wife. Females were not excluded from the events; Agnes Harragin, one of the first licensed female guides in Jasper, was among the regular female participants in subsequent Jasper rodeos.

From 1929 to 1969, the Jasper Rodeo was held south of town at the lower end of the road leading to the tramway. In 1977, the rodeo moved indoors and by 1991 had become a professional event that attracted cowboys from throughout western Canada. Today, the spectacle takes place mid-August at the Jasper Activity Centre, with a packed schedule of other Western-oriented events hosted throughout town that same weekend.

deadfall and overgrowth in its path. With the arrival of the railway, fires became more frequent, and to the untrained eye, they appeared to destroy the landscape. As a result, fire guardians were dedicated to preventing the spread of forest fires. Park management believed that dense green coverage over much of the land was picturesque and what tourists expected to see.

Jasper's annual report for 1924 noted the following fire statistics: "There were a total of 18 fires this year. Fourteen of those fires were caused by sparks from locomotives, three were due to causes unknown, and one was caused by a carelessly discarded cigarette or match. In total, 112 acres of land was burned. The total cost of suppressing these fires was $116.05."

In other years, local residents were awarded cash for extinguishing small fires on their own. In 1925, three Jasper girls each received a cash award of $1.00 for extinguishing a small forest fire. Colonel Rogers wrote in his report to the park commissioner that "the prompt action of these girls saved what might have been a very serious fire. I think it well to pay them 2-hours work for the same as an encouragement to the younger generation to take an interest in preserving the timber assets of Jasper Park from fire, and trust you will approve."

Although Jasper had been referred to as a national park for much of its existence, the designation became official with the implementation of the Parks Act of 1930. In conjunction with the official name change, park boundaries were also altered; an area of 2,538 square kilometres south of Sunwapta Pass was transferred to Banff National Park (which had previously been known as Rocky Mountains Park).

Today, skiing and snowboarding are among the most popular winter sports in Canada, but this is a relatively recent phenomenon. According to a story handed down through generations, Roy Hargreaves was the first person in Jasper to have skis after making his own in 1913. Other locals who were among the earliest to ski included Fred Brewster, Vern and Doug Jeffery, Joe Weiss, and Pete Withers.

After attending high school in Revelstoke, Vern and Doug Jeffery returned to Jasper in 1922 with snow skis. That same year, with their friend Pete Withers, they made the first known ski trip to Maligne Lake. The Jeffery brothers, Pete Withers, and Fred Brewster were founding members of the Jasper Ski Club. Membership in the club grew quickly as the popularity of winter events increased. Gatherings were held at either Patricia Lake or Pyramid Lake. Skiers took turns being pulled across the frozen lakes by horse or car—at the time, it was the closest thing in Jasper to the thrill of downhill skiing.

Although the club focused on events around the town, its more adventurous members regularly skied into the Maligne Valley; Withers later wrote, "Based on the combined experience of these trips, covering a period which includes twelve winters, the general consensus of opinion is that the stretch of country from Maligne Lake, (including the Shovel Pass and Little Shovel) over the [Henry] McLeod Glacier to the Poboktan Summit and Jonas Shoulder gives a better combination of good qualities than any other country skied over. It includes every kind of slope from the 'nursery' variety at the lower end of Maligne Lake to the 1000-foot slopes of the [Henry] McLeod Glacier, and has the advantage of being a direct winter route to the Icefield and Banff."

The club also hosted cross-country skiing races. There were street races for men and women and, for the more advanced, a marathon race. The marathon course began at Maligne Canyon, and competitors made their way over 20 kilometres to Medicine Lake. Then it was downhill all the way as the skiers made their way back to town. The event even attracted skiers from out of town; Paul Gotaas of Camrose was the winner for three years running.

In January 1930, the Jeffery brothers, Pete Withers, Joe Weiss, and Frank Burstrom made an epic winter trip between Jasper and Banff with the goal of reaching Banff in time for the town's Winter Carnival. The men had spent the previous summer placing caches of dried food along their planned route. Taking turns pushing a path through snowdrifts and enduring temperatures as

From left to right, Pete Withers, Frank Burstrom, Doug Jeffery, and Vern Jeffery en route to Lake Louise from Jasper.

low as 40 degrees below zero, the group averaged an impressive 25 kilometres each day. Word of the Jasper skiers and their epic journey travelled quickly. After they passed the Columbia Icefield, two Banff park wardens skied out to meet them and offered their cabin—the opportunity to get out of the cold would have been much appreciated.

The next day, the group members pushed their limits and skied an extra eight kilometres on top of their usual 25 in an effort to reach a warden cabin at Waterfowl Lake. They needed a good night's sleep in order to be ready for Bow Pass, perhaps the most difficult stretch of their trip. After they had reached the summit of the pass, they decided to call it a day and take a much-needed rest.

When they eventually reached Lake Louise, they were greeted by their Jasper friend Jack Brewster and a flurry of newspaper photographers. They arrived in Banff to the cheers of carnival goers who had lined Banff Avenue in anticipation of their arrival. According to Joe Weiss's account of the trip, he found his first night in Banff to be uncomfortable: "The cold spell broke on our

Curling

Curling has been a popular winter pastime in Jasper since the 1920s, local residents of Jasper began to discuss starting a curling club as early as 1923, and the Jasper Curling Club was officially registered in 1925. Mr. Kinnear, manager of the Imperial Bank, was the club's first president and Donald Shorey McCready was its first Secretary-treasurer. In the fall of that year, construction began on a three-sheet indoor rink on the present-day site of the Jasper Aquatic Centre. In January, 1926, Jasper hosted its first bonspiel at the new rink. The rink served curlers until 1949, when a new indoor rink was built across the road. This facility was used until 1975, when the curling rink was relocated back across the road to the Jasper Activity Centre, which opened in May, 1977 and was extensively renovated in 2011.

last lap of the trip that was between Lake Louise and Banff. We arrived at our destination on January the 30th and booked in at the Mount Royal Hotel, hoping for a real night's sleep, but alas, we did not get the sound sleep we had hoped for, in spite of all the windows wide open, it was far to[o] warm for our comfort, we left the hotel to spend the night in the open spaces!"

Curly Phillips, one of Jasper's original guides, took up skiing in 1936 at the ripe old age of 52. Along with Vern and Doug Jeffery and Joe Weiss, he built the Shangri La cabin high above the

Maligne Valley. Far from any road and in the heart of a snow-filled bowl, the cabin was the perfect location for skiing. The foursome dubbed themselves the Maligne Lake Ski Club, claimed Shangri La as their clubhouse, and named the surrounding area Snowbowl. The Maligne Lake Ski Club began offering guided winter trips to their cabin; the adventure cost $30 and included a week of lodging, meals, and transportation from town to Medicine Lake.

Unfortunately, it was Curly's love of skiing that lead to his death. In 1938, he and two young brothers, Alan and Reginald Pugh, set out for Elysium Pass in search of a location to build another cabin. As they approached the pass, Alan stopped to adjust his skis while Curly and Reginald continued forward. In a matter of seconds, the tracks ahead of Alan disappeared in a silent but swift avalanche. Alan later wrote, "The slide came off Elysium Mountain in a main body, approximately 300 yards wide, catching both Curly and Reg. After the slide stopped, I went back to look for them, but found no trace. I called but received no answer."

Word quickly spread throughout the park that there had been an avalanche and Curly and one of the Pugh boys were missing.

In 1927, Merle Brewster, the wife of outfitter Jack Brewster, opened a log tea room at Maligne Canyon (pictured). It was replaced by a larger building in 1963 and continues to serve the many thousands of tourists who visit the canyon each summer.

Looking south across the townsite of Jasper, 1930s.

The town immediately banded together; search parties were sent out and other people stayed behind to comfort the Phillips and Pugh families. The search lasted a week before Reginald's body was recovered, and another week went by before Curly's body was found. It was a sad time for all of Jasper. Fortunately, Curly's legacy remains in the park today through Maligne Lake boat tours and Shangri La cabin.

During the 1930s, as the Great Depression cast its shadow across the continent, unemployment rates in Canada rose as high as 30 percent; in Jasper, many of the newly unemployed had been

Charles Bedaux (standing) and companions during his time in Jasper National Park.

Charles Bedaux

French-born explorer Charles Eugene Bedaux (1886–1944) was one of the most interesting people to ever pass through Jasper. He sold himself as a management consultant and made himself a fortune by increasing employee efficiency for manufacturers. However, Bedaux's first love was adventure. His most ambitious adventure was an attempt to travel from Edmonton to Telegraph Creek, located on British Columbia's remote northwest coast, along an uncharted, trail-less route.

employees of the CNR. While many local families looking for work left Jasper during the Great Depression, others turned to the federal government and were offered a variety of construction and infrastructure jobs in exchange for clothing, meals, and a monthly allowance of $5. Men who were not from Jasper were housed in a simple camp near Lake Annette. Within townsite limits, the workers graded roads, planted trees, and built sidewalks. They were also involved in the construction of a new residence for the park superintendent. The plans submitted by the architect, Alfred Calderon (who designed the administration building),

In the tradition of the Earl of Southesk, Bedaux's ill-fated expedition is remembered more for who and what he travelled with—his wife, his mistress, Academy Award-winning cinematographer Floyd Crosby, two government geographers, 400 books from his personal library, many crates of Champagne, and the best cuts of beef—rather than the trip itself. He also hired over 100 Albertan cowboys, who in turn brought horses for everyone.

In June 1934, Bedaux organized a two-week training camp in Jasper, with local guide Joe Weiss employed to give instruction in wilderness survival. Weiss led them on an overnight trip to Maligne Lake Chalet, up the lower slopes of The Whistlers, and to the summit of Signal Mountain. However, they also found time to socialize, with Bedaux and his entourage attending formal dinners held in their honour.

Finally, on July 6, 1934, after another grand breakfast banquet hosted by Edmonton's elite, the Lieutenant Governor of Alberta, William Walsh, no less, declared the expedition officially underway. By July 17, they had crossed into British Columbia, and on July 22 they limped into Fort St. John. Half-track Citroens, which had regular wheels at the front and caterpillar tracks at the back, were their main form of transportation; these vehicles had been imported from France. When the vehicles did not live up to expectations, Bedaux had them pushed off cliffs and into rivers, which sensationalized the stories sent to the newspapers that were breathlessly reporting his progress, despite "monumental odds." After four months of wilderness travel, the expedition was called off near Hudson's Hope, on October 17, 1934.

In 1942, while working in North Africa, Bedaux was arrested as a suspected Nazi sympathizer. He was returned to the United States and in 1944, while awaiting his trial, committed suicide at a prison in Miami, Florida. Although Crosby never did make the movie, his footage was used in the 1995 documentary *The Champagne Safari*.

were extensively revised in an effort to save money and by late 1936 the two-storey residence at 510 Robson Street was home to the superintendent of the day, Athol C. Wright. Still providing a home for the superintendent and now recognized as a Federal Heritage Building, the building features a stucco and river rock exterior, and original trim throughout the interior.

The most ambitious road constructed during this period linked Jasper National Park and Banff National Park. Known as the Icefields Parkway since 1974, construction of the Jasper-Banff Highway (or the Banff-Jasper Highway, as it was called by northbound travellers) was a major engineering feat. Work began in September 1931 with a Jasper-based engineering crew setting out from the confluence of the Athabasca and Whirlpool rivers, south of Jasper. It took them four months to reach Sunwapta Falls (which presently takes a little under an hour to reach by car from downtown Jasper); their work had to be halted due to snow as it was mid-winter by the time they reached the Sunwapta Falls.

Although the work was menial and the men worked long days, there was a strong sense of camaraderie among the workers. Ted White, an engineer with the highway project, made note of several characters in his memoirs. There was Malcolm MacDougal, a Maritimer nicknamed "Eggie" because he would eat a dozen eggs for breakfast. There was burly Jack MacDonald who used the baffling expression, "I didn't know the Duke of Wellington had died for us!" White also wrote of "the two Jimmies." They were both Scots, and one, known as the "Black Panther," was a dark and brooding character. The other Jimmy was straight-laced, generally happy, and apparently had a soft spot for stray animals.

Construction of the Jasper-Banff Highway outlasted the Great Depression and carried into World War II. The project had begun with mostly manpower and horsepower, but as the construction progressed and the terrain became more difficult, modern machinery was used more and more often. In 1940, one year after war had been declared, the highway was completed; plans for a grand opening celebration were cancelled due to the war, however,

Logwork created by Japanese internees.

World War II Internment Camps

During World War II, thousands of Japanese-Canadians living across Vancouver, even those who had become Canadian citizens, were relocated to internment camps. Three of these camps were within Jasper National Park, west of town towards Yellowhead Pass, and a fourth was located further west, at the abandoned railway town of Lucerne in British Columbia.

Each of these four camps held approximately 200 men. Although the Canadian government justified the camps on grounds of national security, it is clear in hindsight that these men were not a threat. While interned, they were forced to help build a section of the Yellowhead Highway, upgrade an abandoned railbed into a road, add new road, and build numerous bridges. When not working, the men passed their time playing baseball, planting traditional Japanese gardens, and even expressing their feelings through Haiku poems.

It was not until late in 1946, almost a year after the war had ended, that the government began to remove internees from the camps. Two years earlier, Prime Minister King called for a special commission to determine which men were loyal to Canada. Based on the findings of the commission, internees were either allowed to stay in Canada or were deported back to Japan. In 1988, Prime Minister Mulroney formally apologized to Japanese-Canadians who had lived through the ordeal and to their families for the wrongs that were committed against them.

and the highway opened with little fanfare. In the final push to complete the highway, hundreds of conscientious objectors were employed. These were men who had refused military service but were assigned by the government to work in the country's parks and on road-building projects. The men refused service for a number of reasons but religion was the most common; a large percentage of Mennonites, who were exempt by law, refused.

The Jasper-Banff highway was built quickly compared to the Yellowhead Highway between Edmonton and Jasper. Even though there had been demand for a highway into Jasper National Park from the capital as far back as the early 1920s, the highway was not officially completed until the mid-1950s, with help from Japanese-Canadians held in internment camps during World War II.

Even with Jasper linked to Banff and Edmonton by road, driving to the park in the winter was treacherous. Not until the late 1960s, when Jasper's population was 3,000, was the Icefields Parkway between Lake Louise and Jasper open through the winter. As recently as the 1970s, the highway from Edmonton was often closed during winter snowstorms and sometimes would not be reopened for days. To this day, the parkway closes when winter storms and avalanche dangers make driving the route hazardous.

At the onset of World War II, the government initially employed 159 conscientious objectors (Canadian men who refused military service, mostly due to religion) to work on numerous road projects in Jasper National Park. Their tasks included building the road out to the Fish Hatchery (now known as Sixth Bridge) on the lower Maligne River, cutting a loop trail around Lac Beauvert, constructing tourists shelters and the Jasper-Banff Highway, and upgrading the rough track between Medicine and Maligne lakes. Even after the road up the Maligne Valley had been upgraded, the section between Maligne Canyon and the end of the road at Medicine Lake was a narrow track designated as one-way. Vehicles heading towards Medicine Lake were allowed to enter during even hours; those travelling back to town were only permitted on the road during odd hours. There was a gatekeeper posted at Maligne Canyon to monitor the traffic.

While there was a slight drop in the number of visitors travelling to Jasper during World War II, Maligne Lake remained a popular spot for tourists; in 1940, Fred Brewster wrote that he hosted a record 131 guests. He also remarked that an increase in guests had made it difficult for his packers to keep up with the amount of supplies needed. In order to make the transportation of supplies easier, Brewster employed a crew of men to widen the trail between Medicine and Maligne lakes; although the original horse trail was more like a road after his men worked on it, it was still barely wide enough to accommodate a vehicle. Brewster then rafted a fleet of old Packard touring cars across Medicine Lake and began using them to transport guests and supplies between Medicine and Maligne lakes. With the vehicles in place, travel time between the Jasper townsite and Maligne Lake was reduced to eight hours.

One of the most fascinating stories in Jasper's past is that of a top-secret experiment that took place at Patricia Lake during World War II. In September 1942, Geoffrey Pyke, an inventor and consultant to Admiral Lord Mountbatten, chief of combined operations, suggested that the Allied forces construct an artificial iceberg to be used like an aircraft carrier; it would ensure safe seaborne landings and could be used for refuelling. He proposed that the iceberg, which would measure almost one kilometre long, be levelled off and even hollowed out to conceal aircraft. Pyke named the project "Habbakuk" after an Old Testament prophet (he unknowingly misspelled "Habakkuk").

In early 1943, naval engineers and architects arrived in Jasper to build a scaled-down model of Habbakuk on Patricia Lake. Under cover of a 20-metre-long shelter, a refrigeration system was developed and the ideal ratio of sawdust to ice was perfected. By late 1943, with budget overruns and an unrealistic timeframe for construction of the floating aircraft carrier, Habbakuk was officially shut down. Subsequently, the refrigeration system was

Construction of the Habbakuk took place at Patricia Lake in 1943.

dismantled, and the wooden shelter with remaining refrigeration ducts eventually settled in 24 to 30 metres of water on the bottom of Patricia Lake. In 1988, Susan Langley, research director for the Alberta Underwater Archaeology Society, sank a cairn to mark the historical relevance of the unique site.

Jasper also hosted the Lovat Scouts, a specialized Scottish Highland regiment of 600 men, during World War II. Many of the scouts had never skied, so Jasper was chosen as a training ground to improve their winter travel and warfare skills. The scouts arrived in Jasper on January 9, 1944. From the railway station, they marched down Connaught Drive to their temporary barracks at the Jasper Park Lodge, which had been closed at the onset of war. The men lived in the lodge's staff quarters; the golf clubhouse functioned as the officer's mess and the convention room was used as a dining hall. Lovat Scout Corporal Donald John Mackenzie later wrote:

For a week or so we learned about the essentials of skiing near and about Jasper. Our first instructor was a French Canadian. He said there was nothing to skiing and that he was sure we had slid on ice or snow before as kids. He showed us how to put on our skis and fasten them. Then when we were ready with our ski poles etcetera, he said "follow me." He slid down a gentle bank towards the lake and suddenly disappeared. We followed bravely on only to find our instructor standing on his skis on the frozen lake and really enjoying himself laughing at us as he hadn't shown us how to turn or stop, and each one of us took a header and landed on our back-sides on the snow-covered ice on the lake.

Patrick Langford: A Canadian Hero

English-born Richard (Dick) Langford arrived in Jasper by train in 1911 and found employment as a warden under Alex McDougall. After serving in World War I and marrying Olive Mary Stevens, he returned to Jasper in 1919 and was promoted to chief park warden, a position he held until 1934, when he was transferred to Yoho National Park.

The Langfords had two sons, Patrick and Dennis, born in 1919 and 1928, respectively, and raised them in Jasper. Patrick, the eldest, served as a pilot instructor with the Royal Canadian Air Force at Dunsville, Ontario. In March 1942, he was transferred to Britain and served as a bomber captain. On July 27, 1943, he was shot down over enemy territory but survived. After five months in hospital, he was transferred as a prisoner of war to Stalag Luft III prison. While in prison, Patrick, along with dozens of other Allied airmen, helped dig a 100-metre-long tunnel 10 meters beneath his prison. Patrick's assigned job was to man the trap door covering the tunnel. On March 24, 1944, the men made the largest prisoner of war escape of World War II. Of the hundreds of men involved in the construction of the tunnel, only 76 actually escaped, and most were quickly recaptured, including Patrick Langford, who was subsequently executed. *The Great Escape*, a 1963 movie starring Steve McQueen, was based on the escape attempt.

The sacrifices of Patrick Langford, the only Jasper resident to be given military honours during World War II, are commemorated with a plaque that hangs in the local high school and with a stained glass window in Jasper's Anglican church.

After learning the basics of skiing on the grounds of the Jasper Park Lodge, the scouts expanded their skills on The Whistlers. By early February, they began training further from town and established camps at Snowbowl, Watchtower Basin, the Columbia Icefield, and in the Tonquin Valley. During their time at the icefield, Lieutenant Sydney Scroggie and 30 scouts guided by Stan Peyto became the first to make a winter ascent of Mount Columbia.

When it was time for the Scouts to leave Jasper, they did so with a bang, literally. They had been storing equipment and other personal items at the Otto brothers' Mountain Motors Garage, on the corner of Connaught Drive and Cedar Avenue. On April 20, 1944, just a couple of days before leaving, the garage exploded and everything was destroyed. On April 22, 1944, the Scouts departed Jasper aboard a train bound for Halifax and then returned to England by ship. By that summer, the war plan had changed; they were sent to Italy and never used the skills they learned in Jasper. Scroggie later wrote, "The scouts were made welcome in Jasper. The townsfolk found room for all 600 hundred of them when they were off duty. And when they were not eating cinnamon toast with their hosts, getting to know their daughters, or yarning with exiled Scots like the Watsons, there was the Chaba cinema, big Jan's skating rink, Olsen's drugstore with Doreen, and when their month ration came round, the liquor store."

By the time the Scouts left Jasper, almost all of the accessible peaks in the park had been climbed many times over. There was one mountain, however, that remained unconquered until 1948—Brussels Peak, which can be seen from the Icefields Parkway, south of Athabasca Falls. According to Chic Scott, Mount Brussels was known among the Canadian mountaineering community as "the last of the un-climbables." As far back as 1927, Alfred Ostheimer had contemplated the possibility of ascending Brussels during his summer of climbing around the Columbia Icefield, but he was wary of the sheer rock face and his inability to properly assess a route. Over the years, many attempts were made, but it proved to be more of a challenge than most expected.

In the summer of 1948, American climbers Ray Garner and Jack Lewis reached the summit of Brussels, but their ascent created a climbing controversy, the likes of which had not been heard since Kinney's ill-fated attempt on Mount Robson. They had used modern climbing gear such as drills, pitons, and expansion bolts; for climbing purists, this was nothing short of blasphemy. One of the leading British mountaineers at the time, Frank Smythe, wrote the following of the Garner/Lewis climb: "I still regard Mount Brussels as unclimbed, and my feelings are no different from those I should have were I to hear that a helicopter was to deposit its passenger on the summit of that mountain just so that he could boast that he had trodden an untrodden mountain top." Despite the debate, the records show that Garner and Lewis made one of the last first ascents in the Canadian Rockies.

7 After World War II

After World War II, Jasper, like the rest of North America, experienced a tourism boom as people began travelling and taking vacations again. In the late 1940s, around 10,000 tourists were visiting Jasper National Park annually. Visitation increased dramatically over the next decade, with 130,000 visitors recorded in 1953; around 100,000 of these arrived by train and the remaining 30,000 by automobile.

Along with higher tourist numbers, the park saw a demographic shift in the 1950s. Before World War II, the majority of visitors to Jasper arrived by train and were often wealthy and looking to spend a month or even an entire summer in the park. After World War II, an influx of Canadian families arrived by road in their own vehicles. By 1963, the number of automobiles passing through the park gates annually had more than quadrupled from 1953 to 130,000. As a result of the influx of automobiles a new style of accommodation became popular—bungalow camps comprising private cabins set around a main lodge with a restaurant.

The first bungalow camps in the Canadian Rockies were built in Banff National Park by the CPR in the 1920s, and the first such camps in Jasper soon followed, although it was not until after World War II that this style of accommodation became widespread. One of the first bungalow camps in Jasper National Park was Pine Bungalows. It was built in 1936 where Cottonwood Creek joins the Athabasca River, just south of town. A 1946 brochure shows that the nightly rate was $3 per person, which was more expensive than the Pyramid Hotel (now Whistlers Inn) at $1 but less expensive than the Jasper Park Lodge, which cost $9 or more. The original lease was purchased from the government by Colonel Thomas Walkenden, who designed and constructed the original 25 cabins himself. In 1964, the bungalow camp was sold to the Defoort Family, and then a decade later, the Defoorts sold to the Wasuita family, who subsequently upgraded the original cabins and added new ones.

At the same time that Walkenden purchased his lease, Fay Becker was awarded two similar leases—one for a location eight

Since the early 1940s, road-weary visitors have been stopping at Sunwapta Falls.

kilometres south of the townsite beside the Athabasca River and another at the junction of the Yellowhead Highway and Miette Hot Springs Road northeast of town. Originally from New York state, Becker had travelled west to Montana with a survey party in the early 1900s and by 1914 had established an oil brokerage firm in Calgary. Bungalow camp construction on the two Becker leases began in 1937, and by 1940 both locations were taking in their first guests. The cost to rent a bungalow ranged from $8 to $16 depending on the number of persons. Today, what was originally called Miette Hot Springs Becker's Bungalows is known as Pocahontas Cabins, for its location close to the former coal-mining town, has been thoroughly modernized, and is the only one of Jasper's bungalow camps open year-round. South from town, Becker's Roaring River Chalets, now owned and operated by the Venchiarutti family, has expanded greatly and is renowned for its restaurant.

Also dating to the early 1940s is Sunwapta Falls Rocky Mountain Lodge, along the Icefields Parkway, which opened in 1941 as Sunwapta Falls Tea House. The original owner was

Pine Bungalows opened in 1936.

Bungalow camps have been popular since World War II, including Alpine Village (pictured).

William (Bill) Hayhurst, who had moved to Jasper from Vegreville the previous year. In the following years basic wood-framed cabins costing up to $7.50 per night were added. In addition to running the lodge, Bill guided guests on local trails and Mrs. Hayhurst cooked meals in the dining room. In 1947, a new main lodge was built and the original tea house was converted into guest accommodations. After the death of his wife in 1965, Bill and his daughter Grace continued to run the lodge at Sunwapta until 1973, at which time they sold the business to Kevin Roberts. In 1976, what had become known as Sunwapta Falls Bungalows was sold to Paul and Marion Corlett, who along with their children Christine, Mari, Matthew, and Kaitlyn have upgraded the facility to now offer visitors over 50 guest rooms, a restaurant, and one of the park's premier gift shops.

Overlooking a wide bend in the Athabasca River south of town, Alpine Village opened in 1946 as Kiefer's Kosy Kabins (the lodging was known as Kiefer's Alpine Village in the 1950s), with 30 bungalows spread around the forested grounds. Today, many of

Jasper House Bungalows dates to 1956.

Lake Edith Lodge, 1969

Lake Edith YMCA Camp

In 1922, the YMCA established a camp along the shoreline of Lake Edith. Originally, the lease had been granted to Agnes Laut, a Canadian author who envisaged a lakeside artists' retreat. Despite convincing park officials to agree to a special leasehold of 12 adjacent lakeside lots, Laut's vision was never realized. Instead, she donated two of the leased lots to the Edmonton YMCA. At first, the camp comprised 10 permanent tents with wooden floors and bunk beds, but over time, a log lodge and dining hall were built. In the 1950s, the tents were finally replaced with four-room cabins. The camp was used by both groups and families looking for a wilderness experience with more structure than offered at park campgrounds. Guests would spend their time canoeing, boating, swimming, cooking on outdoor fires, and hiking. When Lake Edith Lodge was at its busiest, up to 100 guests would gather for dinner in the dining hall and then move outside to relax around a campfire. In 1975, the camp hosted its last guests and the buildings were subsequently removed.

the original units have been replaced by much larger chalets, and the owners are Chris and Rena Allin, who purchased the property in 1986 from the Stanko family.

South of Alpine Village on the Icefields Parkway, the 28 cabins at Jasper House Bungalows were constructed by John Woldrich and partners in 1956. One of the many workers who helped

Woldrich was Italian immigrant John Forabosco, who, with his wife Josie, purchased the property two decades later. Jasper House Bungalows is still owned and operated by the Forabosco family.

For its lively dance hall, Pyramid Pines Chalet, overlooking Pyramid Lake north of town, was popular with both tourists and locals both before and after World War II. The original Pyramid Lake dance hall was a converted cabin built in 1922 by Jack Brewster for Thomas Keys. In 1935, Keys sold the cabin to Leonard and Nell Jones, who added a second cabin that provided accommodation and advertised the property as Pyramid Pines Chalet. Guests were charged $25 per week, inclusive of meals and shuttle ride from Jasper Railway Station. A band played at the dance hall every night, with a local all-women orchestra supplying the musical entertainment in the late 1930s. In 1955, the property was sold to the Bokenfohr family of Edmonton and has since gone through a number of ownership changes, with the original buildings—including the dance hall—being replaced in the 1960s. It is now known as Pyramid Lake Resort and is owned by Mountain Park Lodges.

In 1934, the park's first auto-accessible campground was established along Cottonwood Creek, where the town access road branches off Highway 16 at the east entrance to town. This new style of car camping was quickly replacing camping styles of the 1920s, which required horses and guides and a camp cook. Car camping allowed families to pitch a tent beside their vehicle and then enjoy modern conveniences like running water and electricity.

The campground at Cottonwood Creek quickly became popular with vacationers; official records show that around 300 to 400 campers registered annually in the early 1940s. Part of its appeal was that it was just off the highway and only minutes from town. Sites were filled on a first-come, first-served basis. Campers cooked their meals in communal kitchen shelters and enjoyed park-related documentaries at an outdoor theatre. North of downtown, Patricia Lake Campground, which opened in 1935, had paved roads and tiered sites, which allowed everyone lake views. After

World War II, the park's original campgrounds at Cottonwood Creek and Patricia Lake were modified to accommodate travel trailers, by which time Cottonwood Creek offered 225 tent sites and 44 trailer sites. To fill the ever-increasing demand for campsites, Pocahontas and Snaring campgrounds opened north of town in 1955, followed by Wabasso Campground in 1959, Wapiti in 1962, and Whistlers in 1964. Today, all the park campgrounds that opened in the 1950s and '60s remain in operation. In 1954, Patricia Lake Campground was leased to the Hoog family who developed Patricia Lake Bungalows while construction of the Yellowhead Highway bypass around the town of Jasper led to the closure of Cottonwood Creek Campground in 1965.

Although Wally Byam developed his Airstream travel trailers in the 1930s, his business did not really boom until after World War II, when thousands of families took to the roads of North America towing his distinctive aluminum trailers. Byam and his devoted followers travelled across the continent as the Wally Byam Caravan Club International and often included Jasper National Park in their itineraries.

The Wally Byam Caravan Club International at Jasper National Park.

After World War II, while campgrounds and bungalow camps were filled nightly throughout Jasper's short summer season, Jasper Park Lodge remained the park's most popular and best-known lodging. Upon reopening in 1946 after the war, it could accommodate 650 guests. The promotional literature produced by the lodge's owner, the CNR, boasted, "No attempt has been made to improve upon nature except inside the buildings where every comfort and appointment is present that one has learned to expect in a modern, first class hotel." Guests could enjoy canoeing on Lac Beauvert and swimming in a lakefront swimming pool, as well as horseback riding, tennis, and golfing. Many guests stayed on the American plan, which included meals in the main dining room. The lodge even had its own orchestra, which performed nightly, except Sunday, from 9:00 p.m. to 12:00 a.m. In the late 1940s, a double room with a private bathroom cost a minimum of $20 per night, inclusive of three meals. The least expensive private cabin was $34, and the Point and Outlook cabins were $100 and $125 respectively for up to four guests (servants cost an additional $6). It cost $0.50 for a bus transfer between the railway station and the hotel, plus $0.50 for each trunk.

On the evening of July 15, 1952, with the main ballroom filled with 200 guests, the main building at Jasper Park Lodge burnt to the ground. An employee was the first to report flames in the vicinity of the coat check room, but by the time the volunteer firefighters from town arrived, it was too late. Although the main lodge was destroyed, the volunteers, along with the lodge's own fire department, spent the night preventing the fire from spreading to the guest cabins. Although all the guests escaped, Len Peters, an employee who had helped disoriented guests find their way to safety, succumbed to his injuries at an Edmonton hospital a few days later. While the fire was a sad event for locals and the many thousands of guests who had stayed at Jasper Park Lodge over the previous 30 years, plans to rebuild the structure were set in place almost immediately. The new building was constructed in the same spot as the original main lodge using rock, concrete, and

The smoking remains of the Jasper Park Lodge after the 1952 fire.

steel. Over 300 men toiled through the winter of 1952–1953 to ensure that everything was ready for the following summer season. The old lodge had been an eclectic cluttering of mountain and wilderness miscellany. The new version was airy and uncluttered—like a breath of fresh mountain air. Floor to ceiling feature windows allowed sweeping views across Lac Beauvert to distant mountains. Two totem poles carved by Canadian sculptor Arthur Price greeted visitors in the lobby, and the cavernous lounge was anchored by a double-sided stone fireplace.

By the 1960s, Jasper Park Lodge had evolved into the resort enjoyed today, and bungalow camps spread throughout the park were thriving. The biggest change to lodging during this era took place downtown. In 1964, the Whistlers Inn opened at a major downtown intersection that had originally been home to the 1922 Pyramid Hotel. Other downtown hotels to open during this period included the Whistlers Inn (1964), Tonquin Inn (1967), Lobstick Lodge (1968), and Mount Robson Motel (1969).

The original 77-room Lobstick Lodge (a lobstick is a tree with its lower branches lopped off that was used by early Canadian explorers to identify a trail), which has since been expanded to 139 rooms, was owned and operated by a group of Edmonton families who had been vacationing in Jasper since the 1960s and who saw a need for motel-style accommodation. Now under the umbrella of Mountain Park Lodges, the group purchased the Andrew Motor Lodge in 1988 and renamed it the Amethyst Lodge for the beautiful Amethyst Lakes in the Tonquin Valley. Originally opened by the Andrew family in 1958, its original 28 rooms had expanded to 67 by 1968. In 1994, Mountain Park Lodges added Marmot Lodge to its lodging portfolio, and then purchased Pocahontas Cabins in 2002, Chateau Jasper in 2007, and Pyramid Lake Resort in 2012.

Jasper Tramway

For a half century, visitors to Jasper have been taking in views of the Canadian Rockies, the town of Jasper, and the Athabasca River from high atop The Whistlers—all without the exertions associated with reaching a mountain top.

Construction of the Jasper Tramway commenced in the spring of 1963. It was financed by William McGregor and Norm Gustafson; a German company, PHB, provided the construction expertise. Although tramways were common throughout the European Alps, this was the first aerial tramway built in the Canadian Rockies. Unlike a gondola, a tramway comprises a tramcar suspended from a track rope (fixed cable) and pulled by a hauling rope. Each tramcar weighs over 30 tons and carries 30 passengers plus one car operator. The distance from the Lower Station to the Upper Station is over two kilometres; the Upper Station is perched high above the valley floor at an elevation of 2,277 metres.

Jasper Tramway

In addition to the Andrew Motor Lodge, the Andrew family built the Astoria Hotel in 1925, when there were only two other hotels within town limits (the Athabasca and Pyramid Hotels). Originally known as the Hotel Cavell, Paul Andrew sold the Astoria to his brother, George, in 1944. With his wife Violet, and son, Socrates, an accomplished athlete, George lived in the hotel for many years. The Astoria dining room was originally called the Jasper Café, and included an ice cream parlour. Today, the Astoria is still owned by the Andrew family and Papa George's is one of the town's oldest and most reliable restaurants.

By 1939, Paul Andrew had purchased the Athabasca Hotel and by the early 1940s also owned the Pyramid Hotel, which was replaced by the three-storey Whistlers Inn in 1964. Located across from the railway station, the Pyramid Hotel opened in 1922. Originally owned by James and Leila Armstrong then sold to Otto Morin and Cy Davignon in 1924, the hotel was a charming wooden structure with locally quarried river stone lining the lower exterior walls and a front veranda where guests could relax and enjoy the mountain scenery.

Although downhill skiing was popular across Canada by the 1950s, the winter wonderland that was Jasper National Park was not promoted as a tourist destination. In fact, anyone arriving in the park during winter would have found that most of Jasper's attractions and hotels were closed—including the Jasper Park Lodge. Winter was the domain of locals, for whom the off-season was a time to relax after working endless hours over the summer.

When the Jasper Ski Club began looking to develop a downhill ski area, the preferred choice was the lower slopes of The Whistlers as it was close to town and had ideal slopes. The club made an application to the park superintendent, James Wood. They suggested that the cleared runs could serve two purposes. When not being used for skiing, during the summer months, the runs could be used as a fireguard. The proposal was accepted and the club was given permission to proceed. In order to ensure that Whistlers Ski Hill was a modern downhill skiing

The rope tow at Whistlers Ski Hill, 1955.

venue, the club raised funds to hire Peter Vajda, a Hungarian-born ski instructor living in Edmonton, to design the layout. Club members volunteered their time to work on many different aspects of the construction. Timber was cleared off the runs by hand and tent cabins were erected so that skiers could have a place to rest and get warm. By 1960, a chalet-style day lodge designed by architect Gordon Sinclair had been completed. The building featured wood sourced from a sawmill in the Whirlpool River Valley, an aluminum roof, a large stone fireplace built by Jasper local John Forabosco, and a ski shop in the basement that was

Powering Jasper

Originally, the residents and businesses of Jasper received their electricity from the GTP and then, later, from the CNR. Power was generated by two small steam-driven power plants located across the rail lines from the Jasper Railway Station. The electricity produced by the railway companies was purchased by the federal government, who then sold it to private consumers through a town distribution system. By the early 1940s, the CNR was no longer able to supply ever-increasing consumer demand in Jasper and Saskatchewan-based Dominion Electric Power installed a diesel-driven generating plant in 1943.

Due to the rising cost of diesel, hydroelectric power was investigated as a supplement to the diesel plant. Warren DuBois, of Dominion Electric Power,

had investigated the Astoria River, south of town, as a viable power source as early as 1937. A decade later, in 1947, construction began on a dam above Astoria Falls, a powerhouse and generator, and a 1.4-kilometre wooden pipeline linking the two. According to Jim Wynn, who supervised construction, the pipeline was so leaky that "it looked like an agricultural irrigation system." Subsequently, the original wooden pipe was replaced with a steel one.

A leaky wooden pipeline linked the dam to the powerhouse.

By 1955, Jasper power consumption was once again exceeded the generating capabilities of the downtown and Astoria plants and in 1956 a second generator was installed beside the rail line. A natural gas explosion that destroyed the downtown power plant in February, 1974, led to an agreement between Alberta Power, Trans Mountain Oil Pipe Line Limited, and Parks Canada, which granted Alberta Power land north of town for a new power plant. Commonly known today as the Palisades Plant, the new facility was up and running by 1975. In 1990 Jasper's two plants, the Palisades plant and the Astoria were linked with the Alberta electric grid in Hinton, as part of a new agreement with Alberta Power and Parks Canada.

operated by Willy Pfisterer, a renowned Austrian alpinist who had settled in Jasper. Despite protests from many locals, in 1969 the government announced plans to close the ski area and restore the area to its natural state. The rope tows were subsequently removed and the day lodge was converted to a YMCA hostel. The building is now leased by Hostelling International and provides budget accommodations for travellers from around the world. (Although the area is now overgrown, the original runs can still be made out above the Whistlers Hostel.)

Marmot Basin

Although ski runs down the lower slopes of The Whistlers were a popular place for winter recreation, as early as 1937, a number of local skiers, including Joe Weiss, had discovered a natural basin filled with snow further south. Known to locals as Marmot Basin, it remained undeveloped until 1951, when Bill Ruddy and Tom McCready were granted a licence to transport skiers to the top of the basin on snowmobiles. The government constructed a road to the base of the basin, and in 1964, the first lifts were installed at what has grown to become one of the major alpine resorts of the Canadian Rockies.

Throughout the 1950s, access to the ski slopes of Marmot Basin was by covered snowmobile.

8 Recent Times

One of the biggest changes Jasper National Park has experienced in recent years regarding tourism is a shift in how visitors spend their time. Traditionally, horseback riding, boat tours, fishing, and soaking at Miette Hot Springs were the most popular activities within the park. Today, hiking is the main draw. In a 1959 government brochure titled *Trail Outings at Jasper*, the hiking trail system depicted is similar to the one enjoyed by park visitors today. At this time, before the Jasper Tramway was built, the trail to the summit of The Whistlers started at the west end of Bonhomme Street and crossed the Miette River west of downtown; it followed a road originally built to the Whistlers ski area. The brochure notes that an optional return to town can be made via the Rodeo Grounds and Kiefer's Alpine Village. The Mina-Riley Lake Loop is noted as being a "new trip," and the trail to Saturday Night Lake is described as "one of the more favourite all-day outings in the park." Maligne Canyon has always been one of the park's most popular attractions; at the time when *Trail Outings at Jasper* was published, Maligne Canyon Road passed between Lakes Annette and Edith, before switchbacking up to the top of the canyon. The trail along Maligne Canyon down to the Athabasca River has changed little in the last century although what was then known as the Hudson's Bay Trail is best known today as the Overlander Trail.

Today, outdoor enthusiasts have over 1,200 kilometres of trails to choose from in Jasper National Park. In the 1970s, Parks Canada began an extensive program of trail building and upgrading. The Tonquin Valley, where Percy Goodair was fatally mauled by a grizzly bear in 1929, and the Skyline Trail, which was pioneered by Fred Brewster and is home to the restored Shovel Pass Lodge, are among the most popular backcountry overnight trips in the Canadian Rockies. You can still reach the Athabasca Pass along the same trail used by David Thompson in 1811, but it is a long, tedious trip along an overgrown trail that sees little traffic. The system of hiking trails in Jasper National Park continues to evolve. One of the most recent additions is the Discovery Trail, which

Jasper National Park Superintendents

1907–1908	Administered by deputy minister in Ottawa
1908–1909	Howard Douglas*
1909–1912	John W. McLaggan*
1912	Byron Burton*
1912 –1914	Samuel Maynard Rogers
1914–1915	Nicholas Charles Sparks*
winter of 1915–1918	Duncan W. Johnston*
1916–1917	Alfred Driscoll*
1919–1929	Samuel Maynard Rogers
1929–1931	Richard H. Knight*
1931–1934	Samuel Maynard Rogers*
1934-1938	Athol C. Wright
1938-1948	James A. Wood
1949-1956	Harry L. Dempster
1956-1960	John A. Pettis
1960-1963	James (Jim) H. Atkinson
1963-1966	Kenneth Bruce Mitchell
1967	Lawrence (Larry) T. Pout
1967-1969	Dennis H. Williamson
1970-1972	James C. Christakos
1972-1983	Rory T. Flanagan
1983-1989	George A. Balding
1989-1996	Gaby Fortin
1990-1996	Michel Audy*
1996-2007	Ron Hooper
2007-2015	Greg Fenton
2015-present day	Alan Fehr

*Acting superintendent

George Balding

Kenneth Mitchell

Fred Brewster's Jasper home is one of many historic residences along and in the vicinity of Pyramid Lake Road.

was completed in 2008. A joint venture between Parks Canada, the town of Jasper, and the Friends of Jasper National Park, with the Jasper Yellowhead Historical Society providing historical interpretation, it comprises an eight-kilometre loop that encircles the town. Formed in 1983, the non-profit Friends of Jasper National Park has worked on restoration of the trail system in the Cavell Meadows and restored Pyramid Lake Island to its natural state.

One of the most-respected and best-known designations in the world is the UNESCO (United Nations Educational, Scientific and Cultural Organization) World Heritage List. On December 23, 1983, a nomination submitted by the federal government for the four continuous Canadian Rockies national parks (Jasper, Banff, Yoho, and Kootenay) was officially accepted. The initial evaluation stated, "Although the nominated site is of substantial size (only four existing World Heritage Sites are larger), it should be noted that only Federal national park land is included. Several of the most outstanding features of the Canadian Rockies (e.g., Mt. Robson, Mt. Assiniboine, Kananaskis, Fortress and

Cuxmins Lakes, and a large portion of the Columbia Icefield), lie in provincial lands immediately adjacent to the national parks." With this in mind, the UNESCO committee urged Canadian authorities to "consider adding several of the adjacent outstanding provincial lands to the site." Subsequently, at a World Heritage Committee meeting in Buenos Aires in late October 1984, with the inclusion of Mount Assiniboine, Mount Robson, and Hamber Provincial Parks, the Canadian Rocky Mountain Parks were officially included on UNESCO's World Heritage List.

As is the case in resort towns the world over, affordable staff housing is an on-going issue. In the early 1970s, a number of lots along Willow and Geikie Streets were leased to the CNR for apartments and multi-family dwellings. At the same time, Fort Point Lodge (now known as Cavell Apartments), was built at 90 Geikie Street. This development was large for the time—161 units over three floors—with businesses such as CNR renting a block of rooms for their employees. The complex was originally designed for singles, with males and females living separately, but today there is no segregation and rentals are open to couples and families.

In the 1980s, Miette Hot Springs underwent a major facelift. The water's healing properties made the springs one of the park's first major attractions; early visitors made the long trek up from the Athabasca River Valley on horseback until a carriage road was constructed. Mine workers from Pocahontas had constructed primitive log pools to contain the mineral-rich water in 1913. In 1934, a more permanent facility was built and road access was upgraded. At this time, around 10,000 visitors soaked in the pools annually. In 1938, what is now known as Miette Hot Springs Resort opened near the hot springs. Originally comprising 10 bungalows, motel rooms were added in the 1960s and chalets in the 1970s.

By the 1980s, the hot springs infrastructure was suffering from structural weaknesses, much of it due to the corrosion of mineral waters on the pipes. Rather than renovate the existing buildings and pools, the new Miette Hot Springs complex was built below

Learn about local history at the Jasper Yellowhead Museum.

Jasper Yellowhead Museum and Archives

The Jasper Yellowhead Museum and Archives, on the northern edge of town at the base of the road leading up to Pyramid Lake, is the best place to learn about the history of the town and the park.

In January 1963, a group of local residents who shared a passion for history formed the Jasper Yellowhead Historical Society. The earliest members included Fred Brewster, Constance Peterson, Ian Coates, Joan Robson, Tom Ross, Nora Findlay, and Roy Fisher. In 1977, the society was officially registered as a non-profit charitable organization. In 1985, a partially completed building on Bonhomme Street was purchased. It was a fitting location as the stables for Curly Phillips's outfitting company were once located on the site.

By early 1992, as a result of many generous donations, hundreds of volunteer hours, and numerous fundraisers, a temporary exhibit space was opened to the public. It was not until 2001 that the museum was completed. Although some of the original members never lived to see their dream realized, the Jasper Yellowhead Museum and Archives has become a place where both locals and visitors can learn about Jasper's connection to the fur trade, the railroad, outfitters and guides, mountaineering, and tourism. In addition to the permanent gallery, the museum has a temporary exhibit space, a retail outlet, and archives.

The Jasper Yellowhead Museum is at 400 Bonhomme Street, a short walk north of Connaught Drive. The museum is open year-round and there is a small charge for admission. Phone (780) 852-3013 or visit www.jaspermuseum.org for more information.

the original, on the site of one of the park's original campgrounds. Completed in 1986, the new complex has two main pools and a large lobby that includes interpretive panels, which tell the story of the springs. Over 100,000 visitors enjoyed the new complex in 1986—an impressive number considering it is a summer-only facility—and today visitation has increased since then by around 50 percent. A short interpretive trail leads up Sulphur Creek to the ruins of the 1934 pool complex.

In 1988, Fred Brewster's Maligne Lake Chalet was added to the Register of the Government of Canada Heritage Buildings, and in 2014 was officially designated as a National Historic Site. The building had remained in use until 1976, when the adjacent day lodge was completed. Today, after extensive restoration and now operated as a restaurant by Pursuit, the beautiful log building stands as a tribute to Fred Brewster and his considerable contributions to early tourism at the lake.

Politically, the biggest change since Jasper Forest Park was established in 1907 has been the incorporation of Jasper as a town, which occurred in 2001. As a settlement within a national park, Jasper was originally under federal government jurisdiction, but by late last century, this had led to tension between residents and Parks Canada regarding everything from hospital facilities to planning issues.

During the 1980s, Jasper's neighbour to the south, Banff, fought to gain municipal status. Finally, on January 1, 1990, through a joint agreement between the local citizens and the federal and provincial governments, Banff was officially incorporated as a town, which made it the first incorporated municipality within a national park. Eleven years later, on July 20, 2001, the town of Jasper was granted the same autonomy; Richard Ireland was elected mayor, with Joe Couture, Mike Day, Gloria Kongsrud, Ross Pugh, Andy Walker, and Brenda Zinck elected as councillors.

Although the town of Jasper operates similarly to communities of a similar size across Canada, it remains subject to the National Parks Act. Although the federal government is the ultimate authority on planning, land use, development, and environmental issues, the municipality is often invited to participate as a partner in planning decisions. Today, the town of Jasper is governed by a mayor and six councillors. Municipal elections are held every three years, in accordance with the Elections Act of Alberta.

As a town in a national park, the residents of Jasper have to be conscious of the impact they have on the surrounding ecosystem. In order to avoid the exploitation of park land, construction and expansion are heavily restricted. The last major residential construction project within the Jasper town limits happened in the 1980s with the construction of Cabin Creek West housing division.

Since incorporation in 2001 and due to a longstanding cap on development, the population of Jasper has remained stable. The official permanent population of Jasper is 4,590 although this number increases significantly each summer, when there is an influx of seasonal workers. As in resort towns the world over, the median age of Jasper residents is lower than in comparable towns, at approximately 31.5 (over half the town residents are aged 20 to 44). And while Jasper has always had a very strong community element, with a core of 2,000 to 3,000 long-term residents, around 15 percent of the permanent population rotates each year—that is, 15 percent of those who leave Jasper are offset by new arrivals. As has been the case for well over a century, people from around the world make their home in Jasper. Today, between 8 and 10 percent of the town's population was born outside of Canada.

Since the first passenger train rolled into Jasper in 1912, the town and the surrounding park have come a long way. Jasper has evolved from a railway construction camp to a world-class, year-round tourist destination. Just like they have for the last century, the natural wonders of Maligne Canyon, Maligne Lake, Miette Hot Springs, and Mount Edith Cavell continue to draw visitors from around the world, currently with upwards of two million visitors enjoying the wonders of Jasper each year. Hiking and biking trails lace the Athabasca River Valley, golfers walk the

The Point Cabin, at the Fairmont Jasper Park Lodge, has been a favourite getaway for celebrities and royalty since 1928.

fairways of one of the world's most scenic golf courses, and in winter, skiers and snowboarders take to the slopes of Marmot Basin. Accommodations range from rustic hostels to upscale lodges, and bakeries, elegant dining rooms, and family-friendly restaurants provide food for all tastes and budgets.

Thankfully, through all the changes that Jasper has seen in the last century, its long and colourful history is kept alive through historic sites, heritage buildings, and collected artifacts. The best place to begin a journey into Jasper's past is the Jasper Yellowhead Museum and Archives. Within walking distance of the museum is Fred Brewster's historic log home and a string of other 1920s heritage homes on Pyramid Lake Road. Downtown, both locals and visitors can immerse themselves in the past by visiting Jasper's oldest building, the Park Visitor Centre; enjoying a drink at the 1928 Athabasca Hotel, or wandering through the heritage-listed railway station. Regardless of whether you are a long-time resident or a first-time visitor, immersing yourself in the town's long and colourful history will only enhance your experience of Jasper.

Jasper Timeline

10,000 BC	Paleo-Indians first visit the Athabasca River Valley
1700s	Local Aboriginal people feel first effects of the fur trade
1811	David Thompson crosses Athabasca Pass
1813	North West Company opens a trading post at Brule Lake
1814	Jasper Haws takes over as postmaster
1829	Trading post is relocated to Jasper Lake
1857	With the fur trade in decline, Jasper House is closed
1858	Henry John Moberly reopens Jasper House
1859	Palliser Expedition member Dr. James Hector explores the region
1859	The Earl of Southesk is the valley's first tourist
1891	Jasper House is officially closed
1907	Dominion government establishes Jasper Forest Park

Jasper House in 1872, as photographed by Charles Horetzky.

1908	Mary Schäffer reaches the shore of Maligne Lake
1909	Railway surveyors reach the valley
1911	Lewis Swift is the park's only remaining homesteader
1911	Railway divisional point established at Mile 112
1913	Settlement is named Jasper
1913	Park Administration Building is completed

Mary Schäffer reached Maligne Lake in 1908.

1922	Jasper Park Lodge opens
1923	Chaba Theatre screens its first movies
1924	Population of Jasper is 400
1930	Jasper Forest Park is renamed Jasper National Park
1940	The Icefields Parkway is completed
1951	Population of Jasper is 1,728
1963	Jasper-Yellowhead Historical Society is formed
1964	Marmot Basin ski area opens
1964	Jasper Tramway is completed
1991	Population of Jasper is 3,567
2001	Jasper is incorporated as a town
2006	Population of Jasper is 4,180
2008	Discovery Trail encircles the town
2011	Two Brothers totem pole raised
2020	Population of Jasper is 4,590

Two Brothers totem pole.

Further Reading

Bickersteth, J. Burgon. *The Land of Open Doors: Being letters from Western Canada 1911–1913*. Toronto: University of Toronto Press, 1976. First published in 1914, this is an invaluable collection of letters for those interested in railroad construction and pioneer life in Alberta.

Hart, E.J. *Diamond Hitch*. Banff: EJH Enterprises, 2001. Hart's *Diamond Hitch* describes the colourful lives and times of pioneer outfitters and guides who had an early impact on the Canadian Rockies, including Tom Wilson, Bill Peyto, Jimmy Simpson, the Brewster brothers, Fred Stephens, and Curly Phillips.

Hart, E.J. *J.B. Harkin: Father of Canada's National Parks*. Edmonton: University of Alberta, 2011. The extensive research of respected historian E.J. (Ted) Hart comes together in this tome that tells the story of Canada's first commissioner of national parks.

Jenness, Diamond. *The Indians of Canada*. Toronto: University of Toronto Press, 1977. Originally published in 1932, this is the classic study of natives in Canada, although Jenness's conclusion that they were facing certain extinction by the end of the 20th century is obviously outdated.

Karamitsanis, Aphrodite. *Place Names of Alberta*. Calgary: University of Alberta Press, 1991. Volume 1 alphabetically lists all geographic features of the Canadian Rockies with explanations of each name's origin.

MacGregor, J. G. *Overland by the Yellowhead*. Saskatoon: Western Producer Book Service, 1974. Although now out of print, this classic delves into the history of one of the Canadian Rockies major travel routes. It contains valuable historic records, including stories that the author collected from Alberta pioneers.

Marty, Sid. *Switchbacks: True Stories from the Canadian Rockies*. Toronto: McClelland & Stewart, 1999 (reprinted in 2008). This book tells of Marty's experiences in the mountains and of people he came in contact with in his role as a park warden. Along the way he describes the way his experiences with both nature and fellow humans have shaped his views on conservation.

Murphy, Peter J. *A Hard Road to Travel: Land Forests and People in the Upper Athabasca Region*. Hinton: Foothills Model Forest, 2007. The most recent and up to date research on the human history of the Upper Athabasca Valley and what is now Jasper National Park.

MacLaren, Ian (editor). *Culturing Wilderness in Jasper National Park: Studies in Two Centuries of Human History in the Upper Athabasca River Watershed*. Edmonton: University of Alberta Press, 2007. A volume of essays that focus on the human history of the Athabasca River Valley and the impact of politics and park management on the landscape of Jasper National Park.

Patton, Brian and Bart Robinson. *Canadian Rockies Trail Guide*. Banff: Summerthought Publishing, 2011. Primarily a hiking guide, the authors include many notes of historical interest regarding early explorers and the trails they blazed.

Power, Meghan. *Maligne Lake: The Jewel of Jasper National Park*. Banff: Summerthought Publishing, 2011. Comprehensive, yet reader-friendly, Maligne Lake tells the story of one of Canada's best-known natural attractions through extensive research, historic and contemporary photos, and interesting sidebars.

Schäffer, Mary T. S. *A Hunter of Peace*. Banff: Whyte Museum of the Canadian Rockies, 2001. This book was first published in 1911 by G.P. Putnam & Sons, New York, under the name Old Indian Trails of the Canadian Rockies. Tales recount the exploration of the Rockies during the turn of the 20th century. Many of the author's photographs appear throughout.

Scott, Chic. *Pushing the Limits*. Calgary: Rocky Mountain Books, 2000. A chronological history of mountaineering in Canada, with special emphasis on many largely unknown climbers and their feats, as well as the story of Swiss guides in Canada and a short section on ice-climbing.

Smith, Cyndi. *Jasper Park Lodge: In the Heart of the Canadian Rockies*. Jasper: self-published, 1985. The complete history of Jasper's most famous accommodation. Includes historic photos and a chapter on the golf course.

Smith, Cyndi. *Off the Beaten Track*. Lake Louise: Coyote Books, 1989. An excellent resource for those wishing to read more about the adventurous women of the Canadian Rockies, including Mary Schäffer, Mary Vaux, the Harragin sisters, and Caroline Hinman. Smith's narrative is easy to read and contains many interesting facts about mountain heroines.

Spry, Irene M. *The Palliser Expedition: The Dramatic Story of Western Canadian Exploration 1857-1860*. Calgary: Fifth House, 1963. Spry's book is one of the first to tell the story of the 1857–1860 Palliser Expedition. The scientists involved in this expedition were the first to study western Canada and the Canadian Rockies.

Taylor, William C. *Tracks Across My Trail*. Jasper: Jasper Yellowhead Historical Society, 1984. The biography of Donald "Curly Phillips, one of Jasper's most well known and loved guides and outfitters.

Index

Photo Credits

Summerthought Publishing would like to thank the following for permission to reproduce their contemporary and archival images:

Glenbow Archives: p. 2 (na-1408-19), p. 3 (na-1679-12), p. 22 (na-568-1), p. 31 (na-3840-5), p. 33 (na-588-1), p. 34 (na-1355-1), p. 39 (na-1408-19)

Andrew Hempstead: p. 5, p. 9, p. 40, p. 64, p. 84, p. 109 (top and bottom), p. 115, p. 151, p. 157, p. 163, p. 166, p. 168, p. 171

Jasper Yellowhead Museum and Archives: p. 1 (pa69-13), p. 4 (994.45.112.3), p. 15, p. 25, p. 29 (84.72.58), p. 37 (pa20-28), p. 47 (bottom; pa22-18), p. 53 (996.38.03), p. 55 (2006.79.72), p. 57 (pa39-20), p. 58 (pa6-50), p. 61 (pa39-17), p. 62-63 (pa39-1), p. 65 (pa46-3), p. 66 (pa6-46), p. 69 (pa6-21), p. 70 (pa7-51), p. 72 (993.36.24), p. 73 (pa41-90), p. 74-75 (pa41-88), p. 77 (993.36.69), p. 79 (999.07.140), p. 81 (pa62-11), p. 83 (pa34-6), p. 87 (pa38-8), p. 88 (pa62-2), p. 90 (pa38-20), p. 91 (pa38-66), p. 92-93 (002.16.01), p. 94 (pa33-31), p. 97 (997.07.77.07), p. 99 (990.57.26), p. 100-101 (2006.79.120), p. 102 (993.37.46a), p. 103 (994.56.1346), p. 105 (994.35.62), p. 106 (993.36.40), p. 108 (pa18-3), p. 111 (001.13.14), p. 113 (992.03), p. 116-117 (001.33.223), p. 118 (2011.85.07), p. 121 (990.63.15), p. 122 (pa41-82), p. 123 (002.16.14), p. 124-125 (pa18-22), p. 126 (89.36.262), p. 129 (994.56.1006), p. 130 (pa34-30), p. 131 (000.34.249), p. 132-133 (996.33.390), p. 134 (994.56.870), p. 137 (pa26.48), p. 140 (84.32.179), p. 145 (991.21), p. 148-149 (2004.49.0893), p. 150 (2004.49.0895), p. 152 (2004.49.0905), p. 155 (998.45.13), p. 156 (999.03.89), p. 159 (89.32.04), p. 160 (994.56.1907), p. 161 (994.56.1079), p. 165 (left; 999.07.429), p. 165 (right; 999.07.428)

Sunwapta Falls Rocky Mountain Lodge: p. 147

Whyte Museum of the Canadian Rockies: p. 7 (v527-ng-124), p. 43 (v527-ps-1-53), p. 44 (v527-pd1-1), p. 47 (top; v527-ps-1-131), p. 48 (v527-pd1-2), p. 76 (v263-na-1157)

Acknowledgments

I would like to take the opportunity to thank everyone who helped with this project; as the author I would like to take responsibility for any errors that appear within these pages. I would like to especially thank Glenda Cornforth, who introduced me to Jasper's history, as well as Tom Peterson, Harry Home, Karen Byers and all the Jasper locals who have shared their personal histories with me over the course of this project. I would also like to give special thanks to Ron Pelletier, a direct descendent of John Moberly, who shared his family's history and was always ready to answer questions about his ancestors. Special thanks also to Mike Dillon and the many Parks Canada employees who were always willing to answer my many questions. Finally, thanks to the Jasper Yellowhead Historical Society and the Jasper Yellowhead Museum and Archives for their unwavering dedication to the preservation of Jasper National Park's history.

About the Author

Meghan Power worked at the Jasper Yellowhead Museum and Archives between 2004 and 2013. During her time there as the archivist, she gained an unrivaled opportunity to learn about the history of the town and park. She currently lives in Banff, designing writing residencies at the Banff Centre for Arts and Creativity.